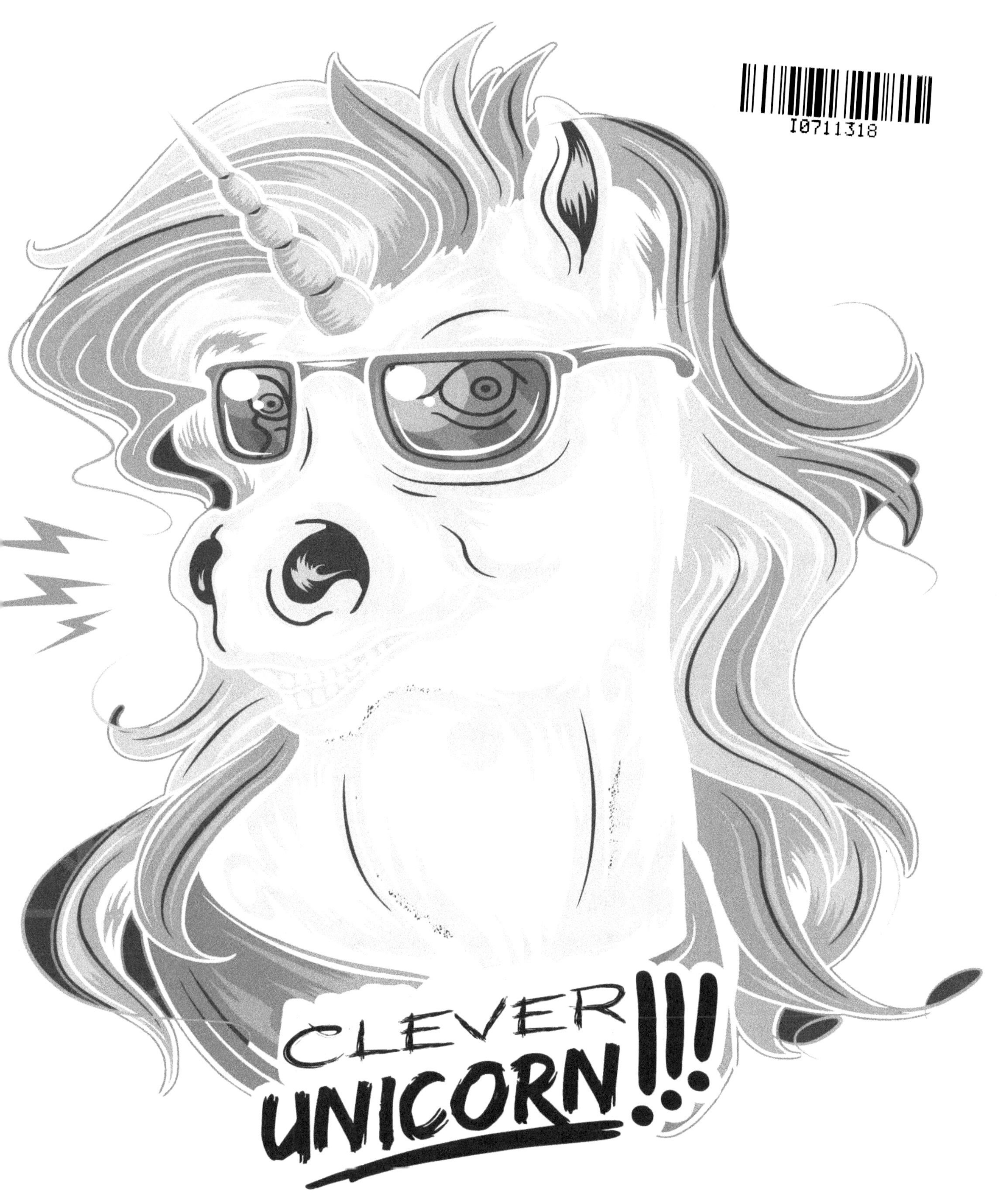

CLEVER
UNICORN!!!

This Book
Belongs To

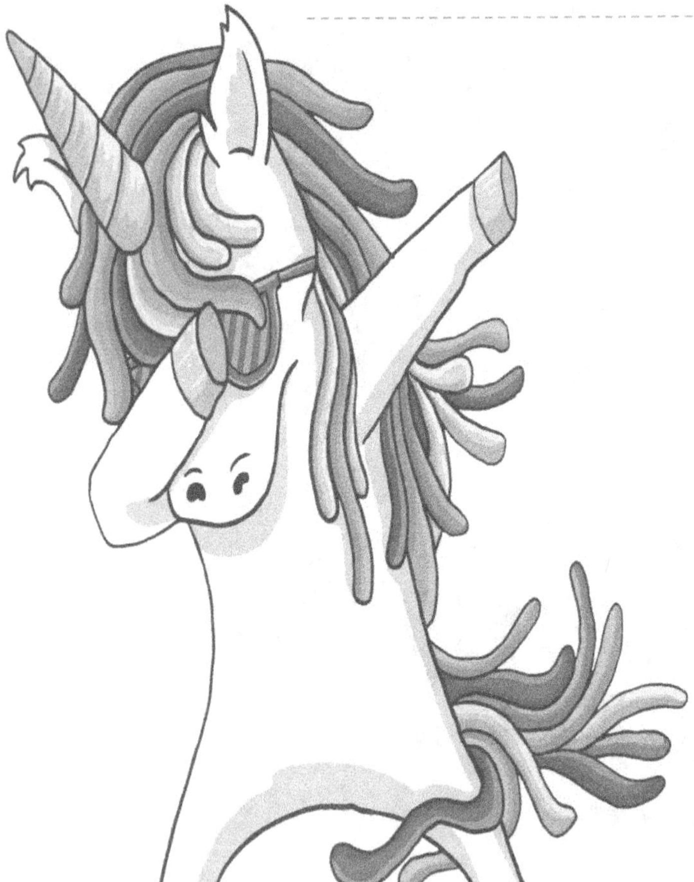

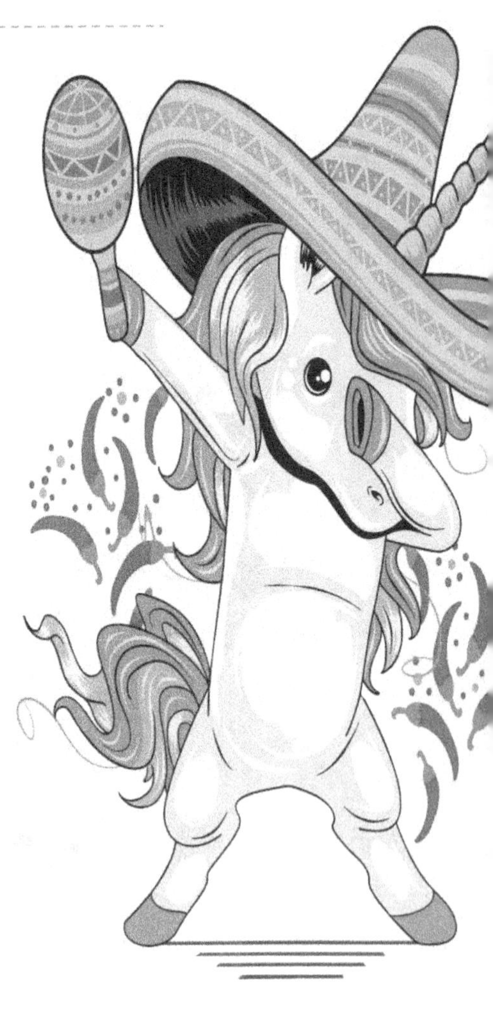

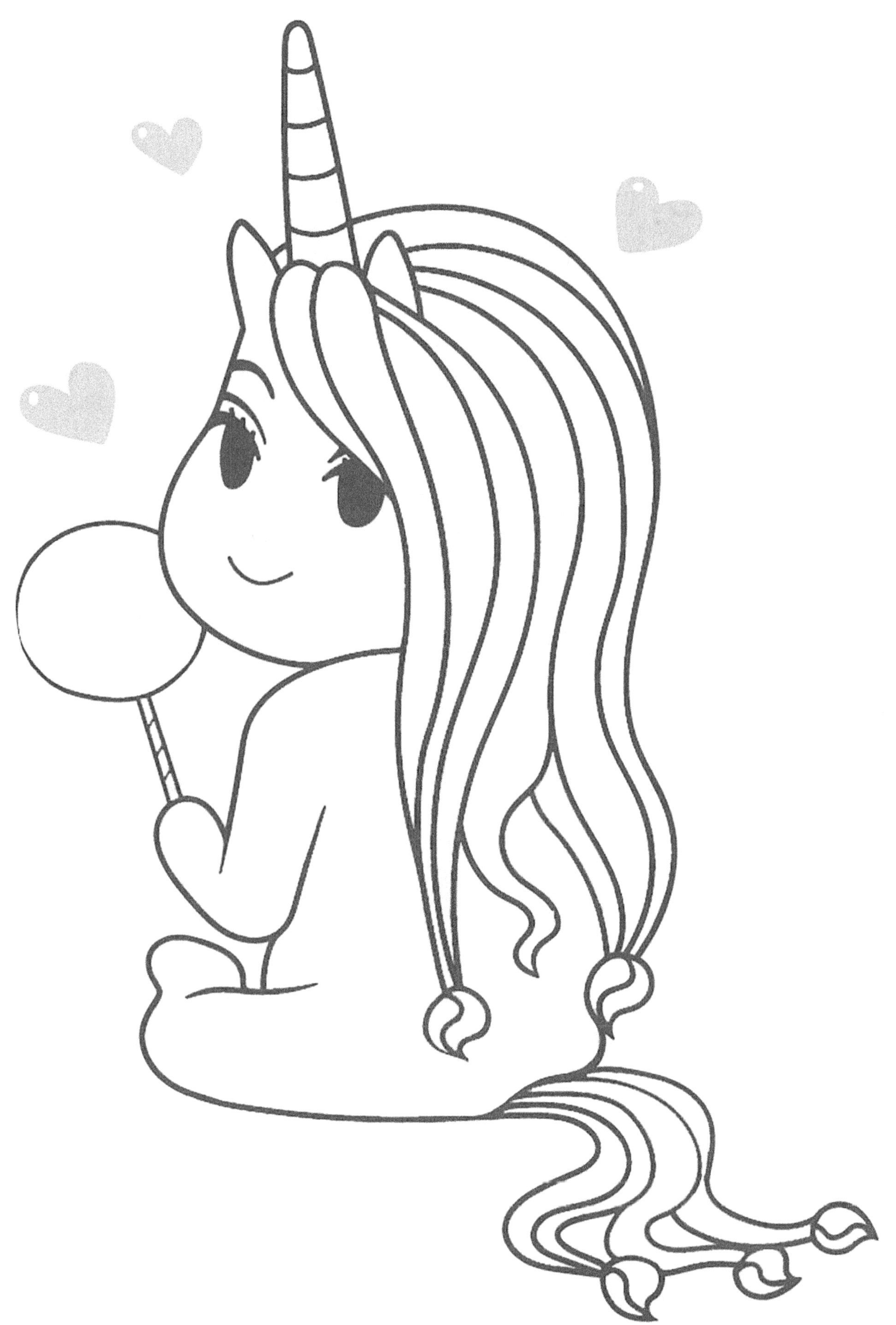

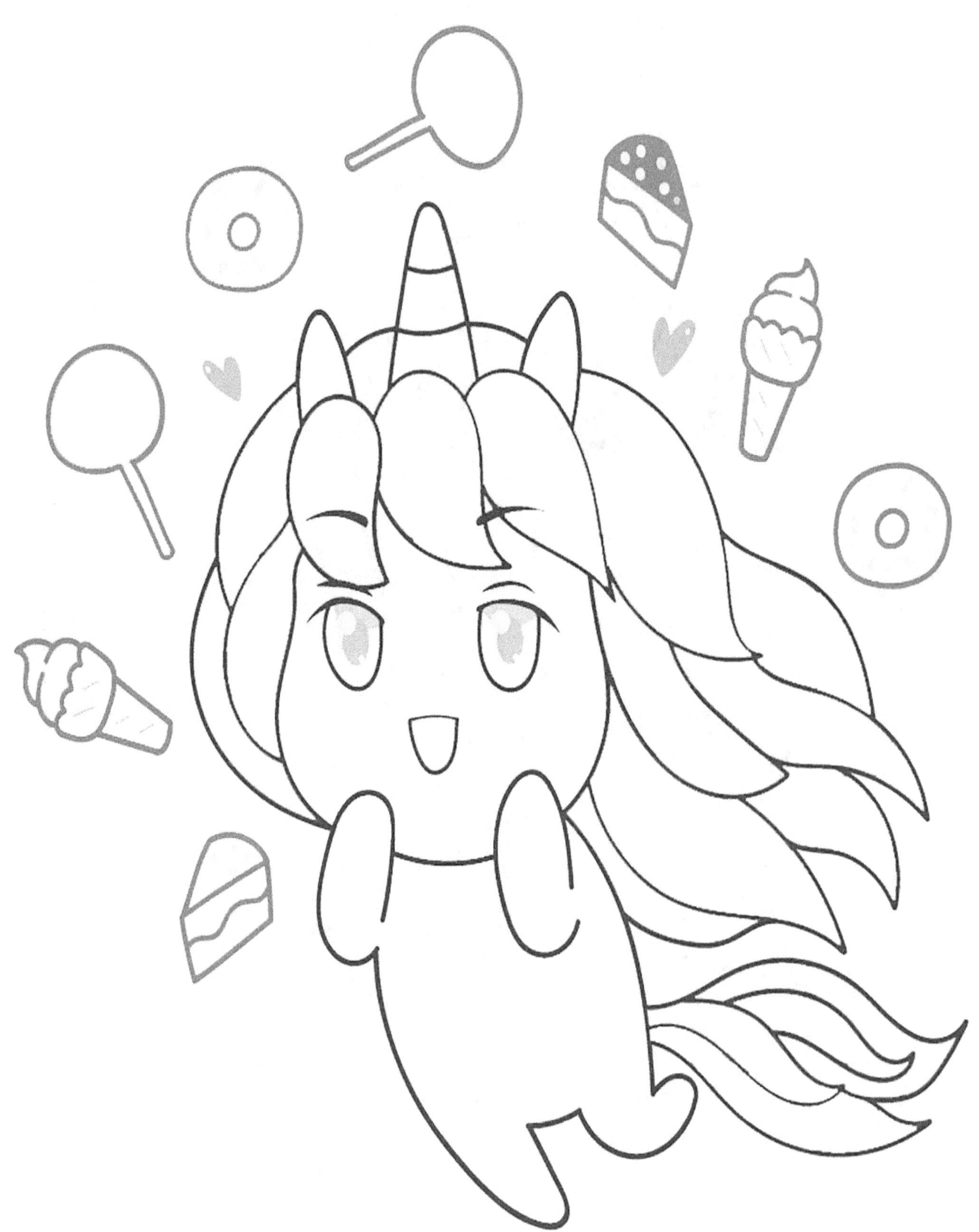

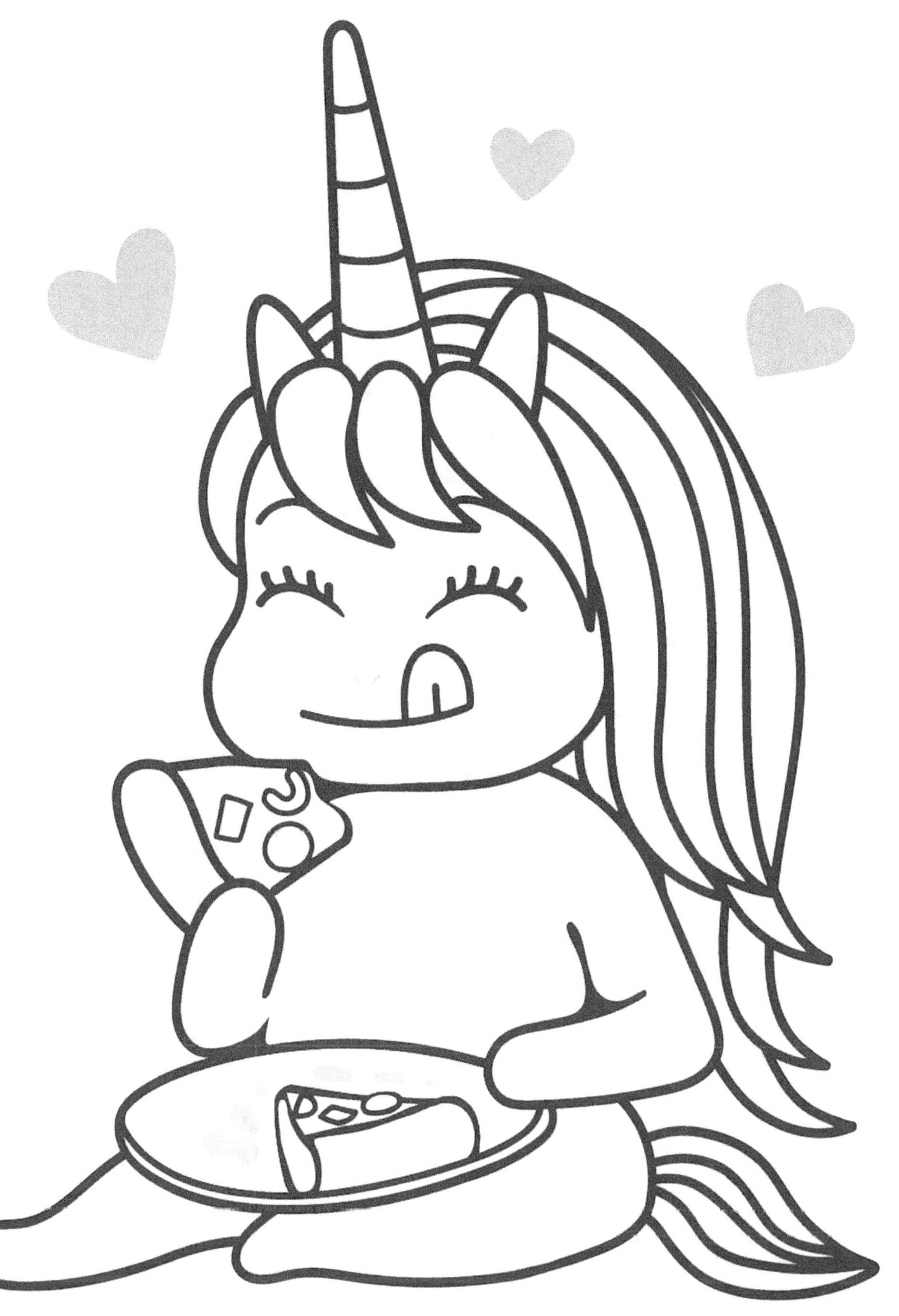

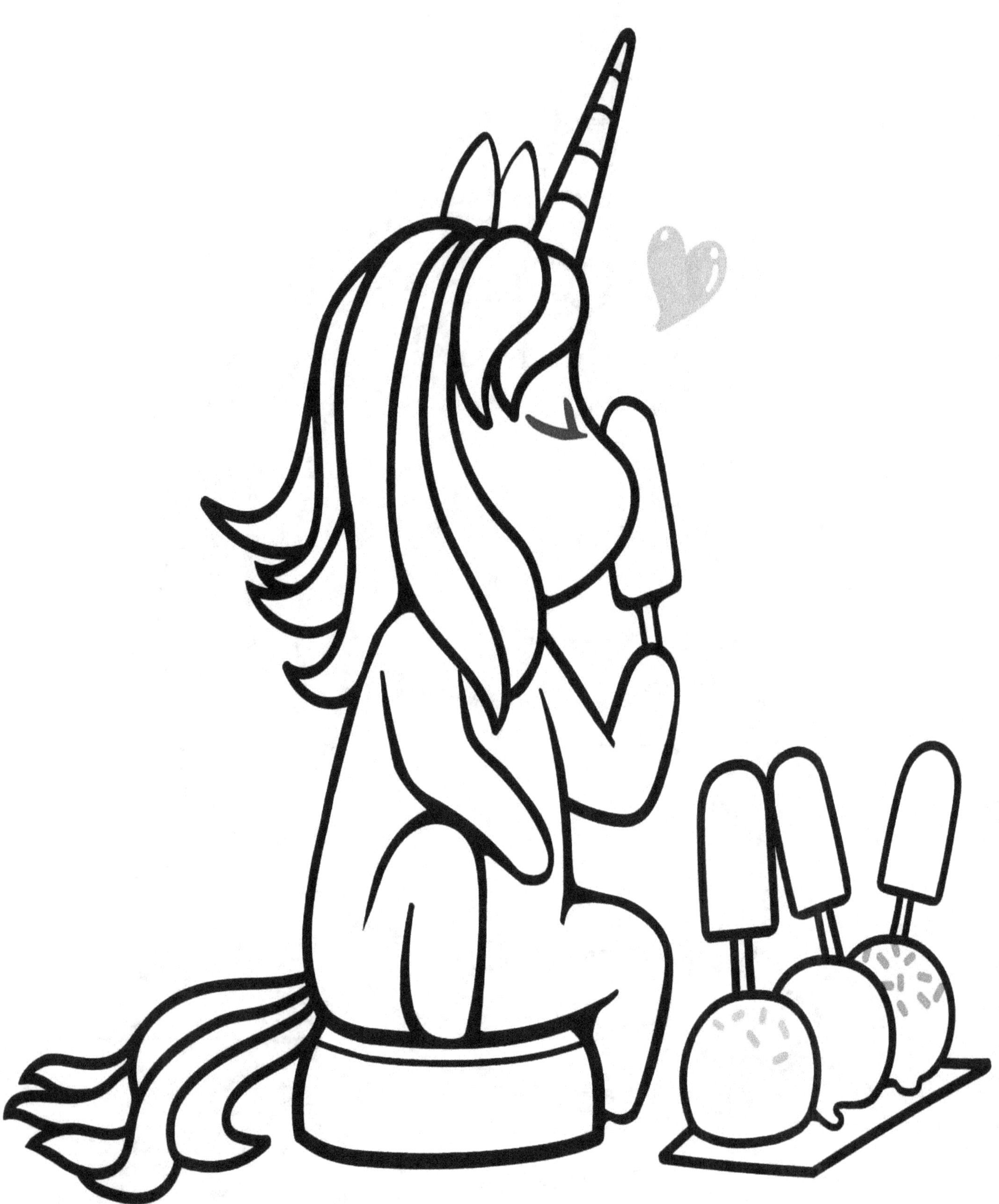

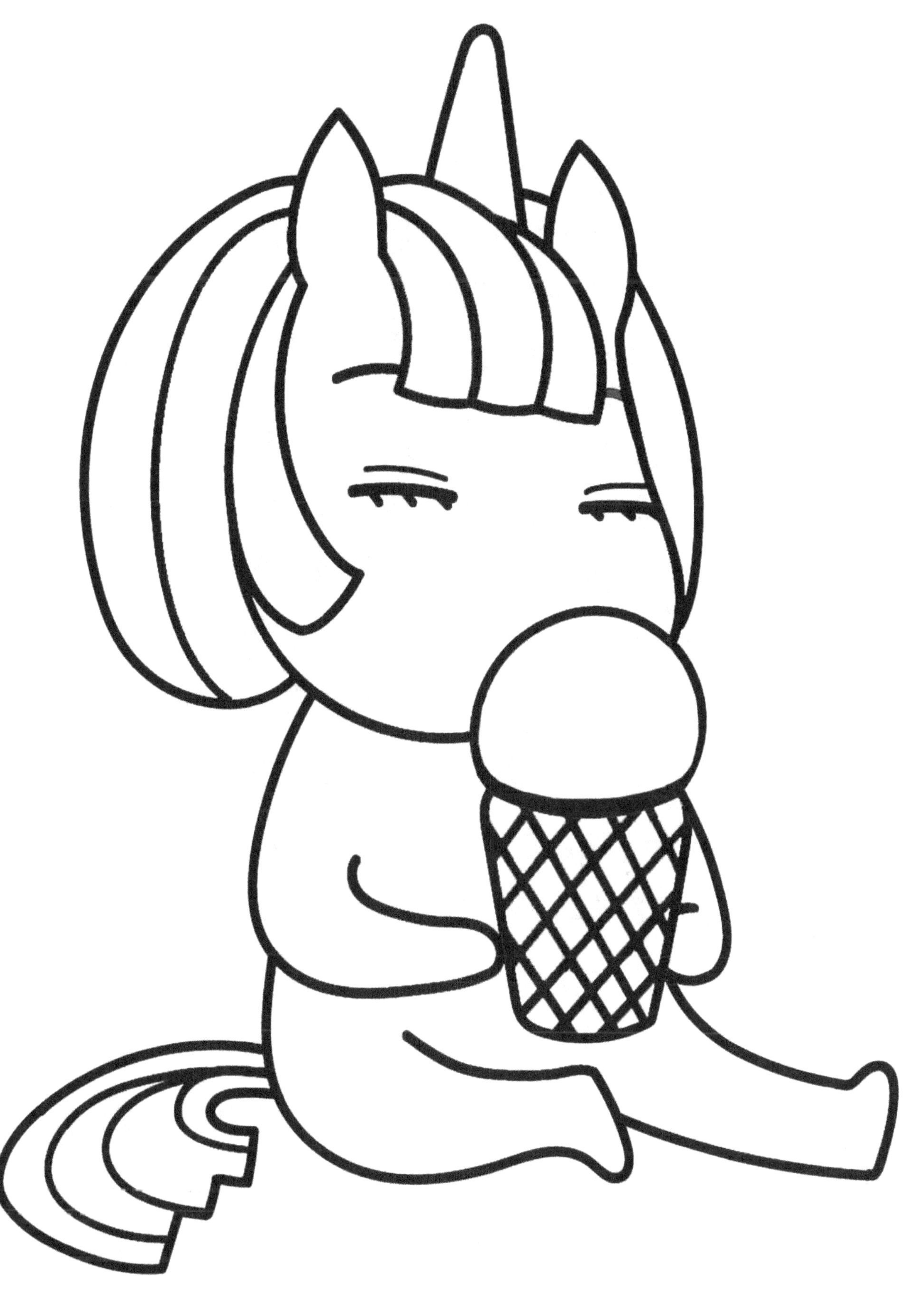

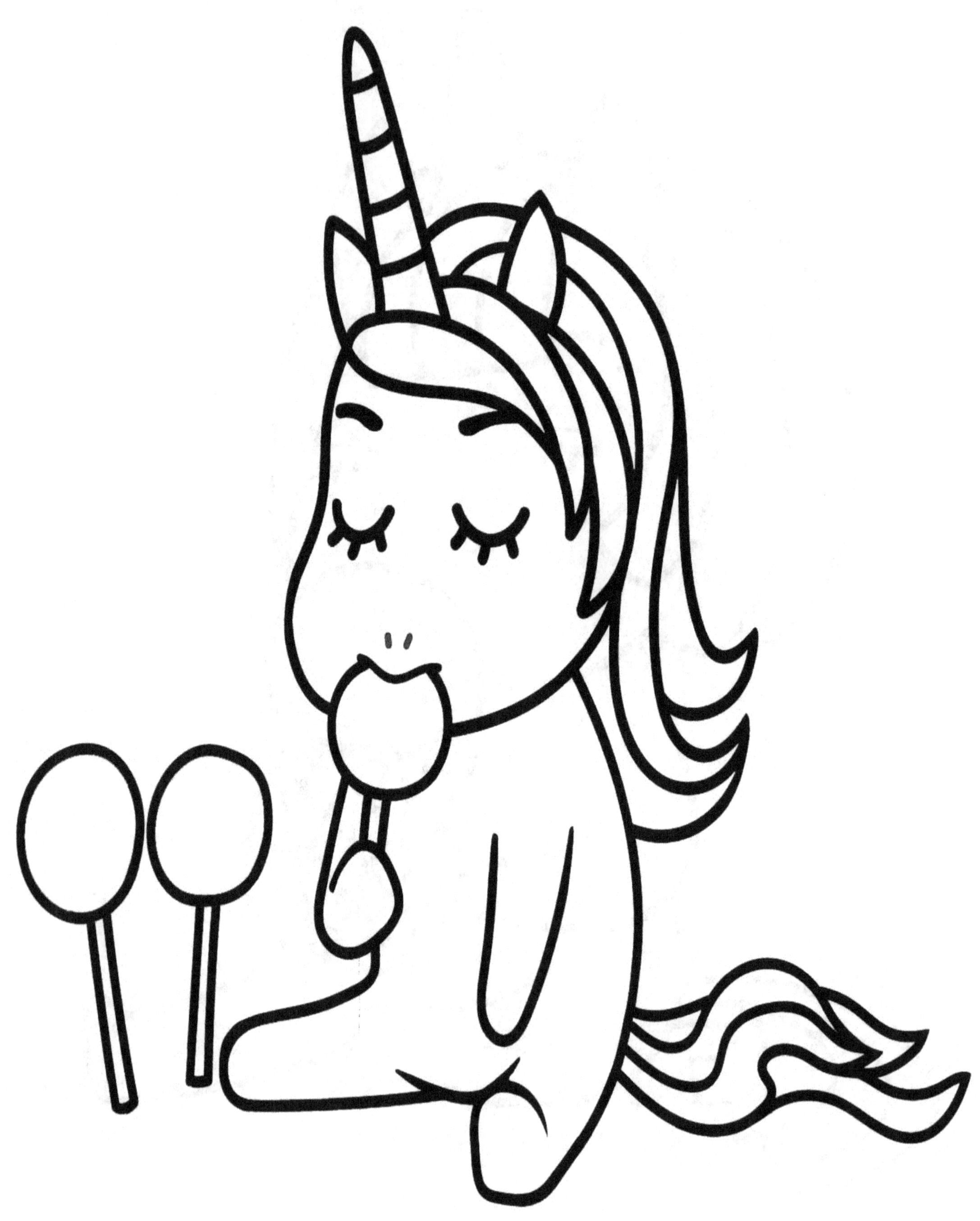

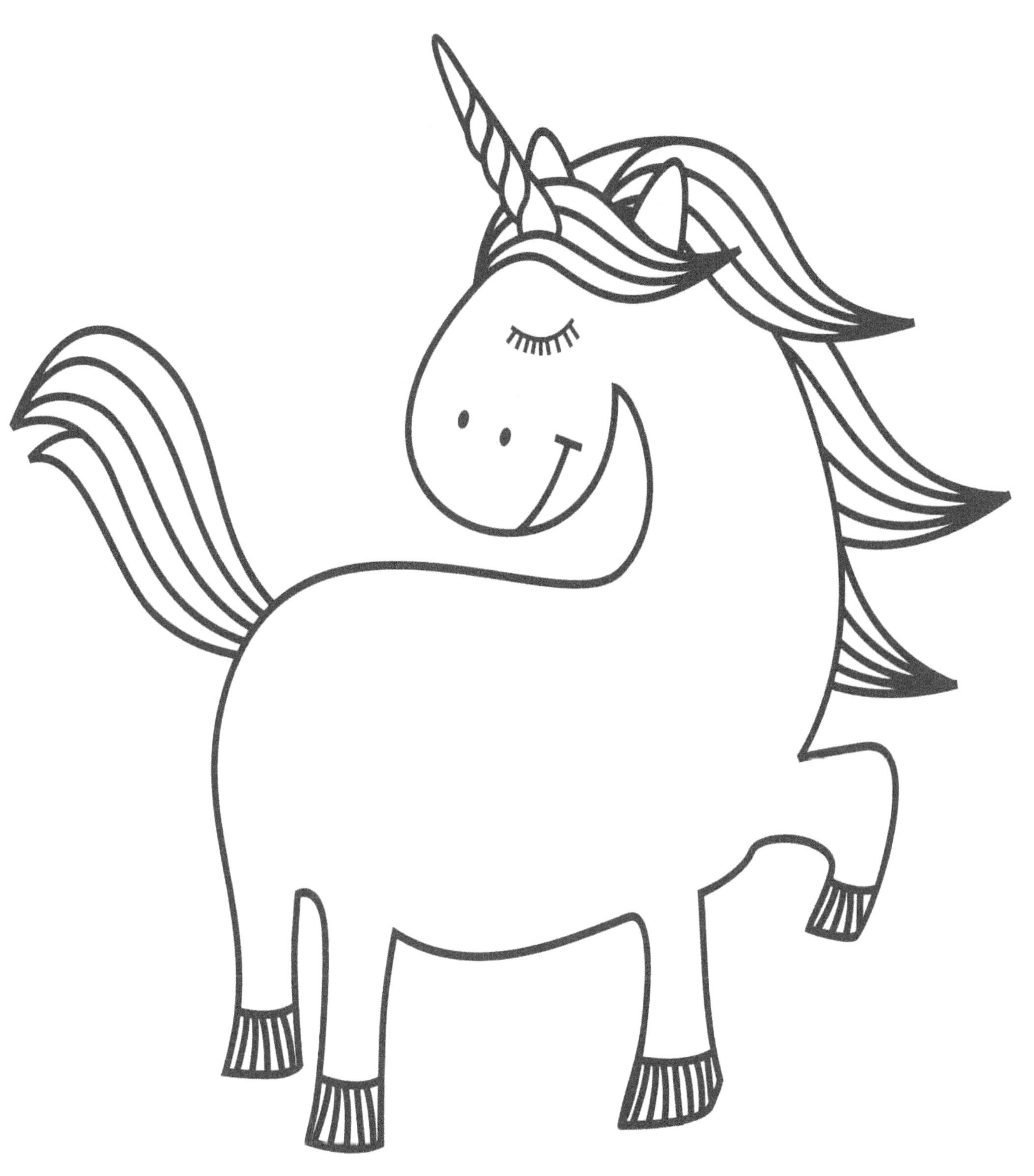

SO CUTE

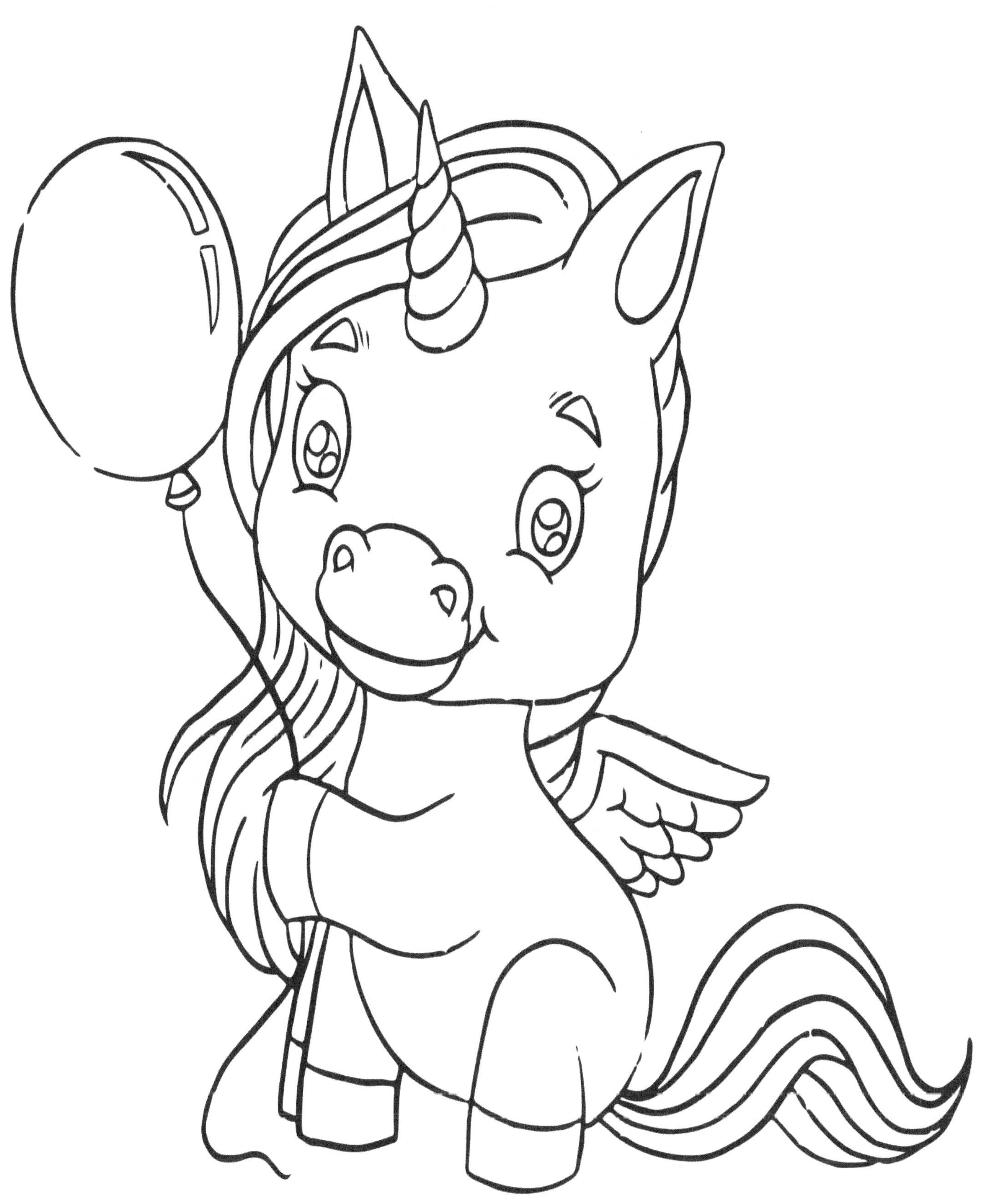

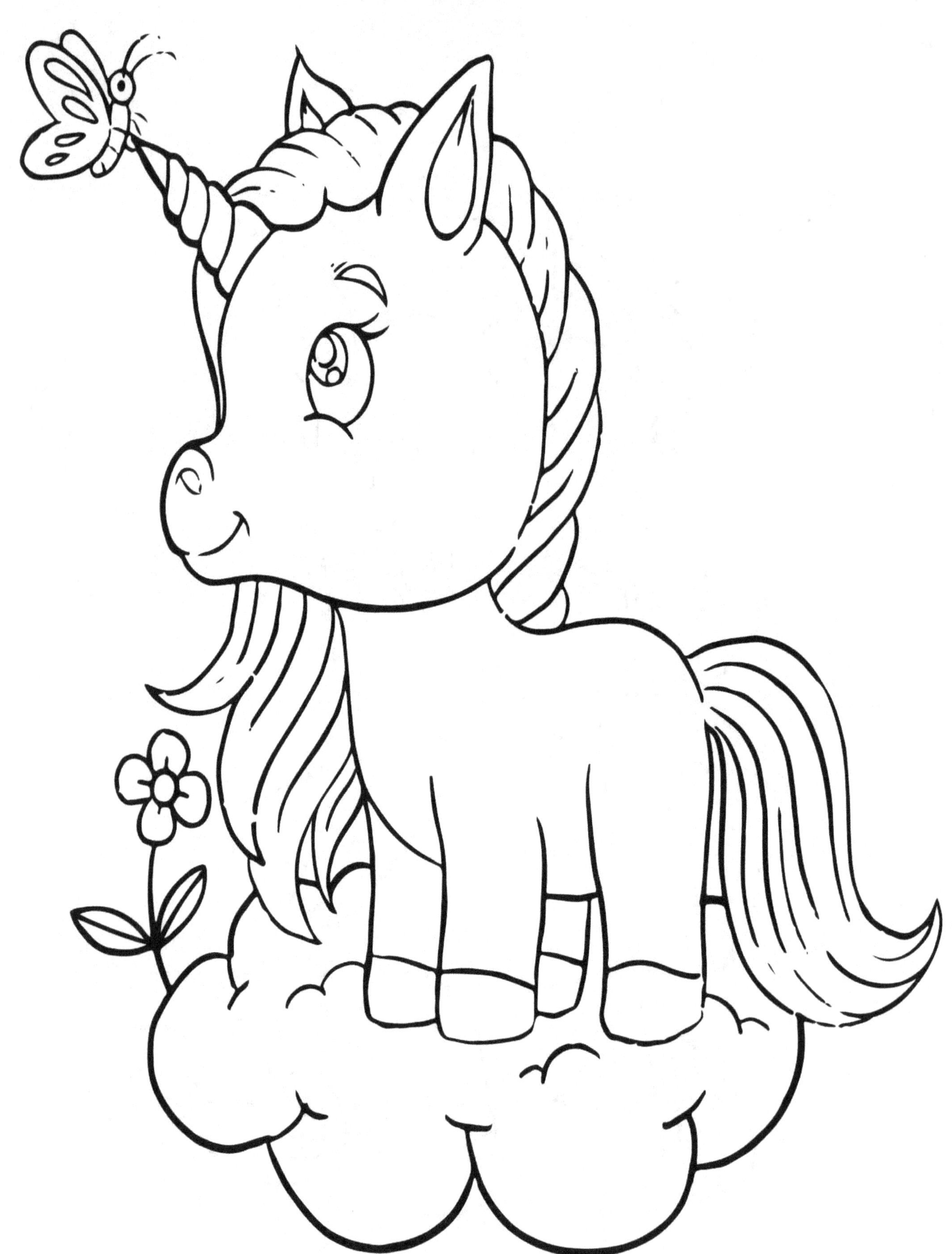

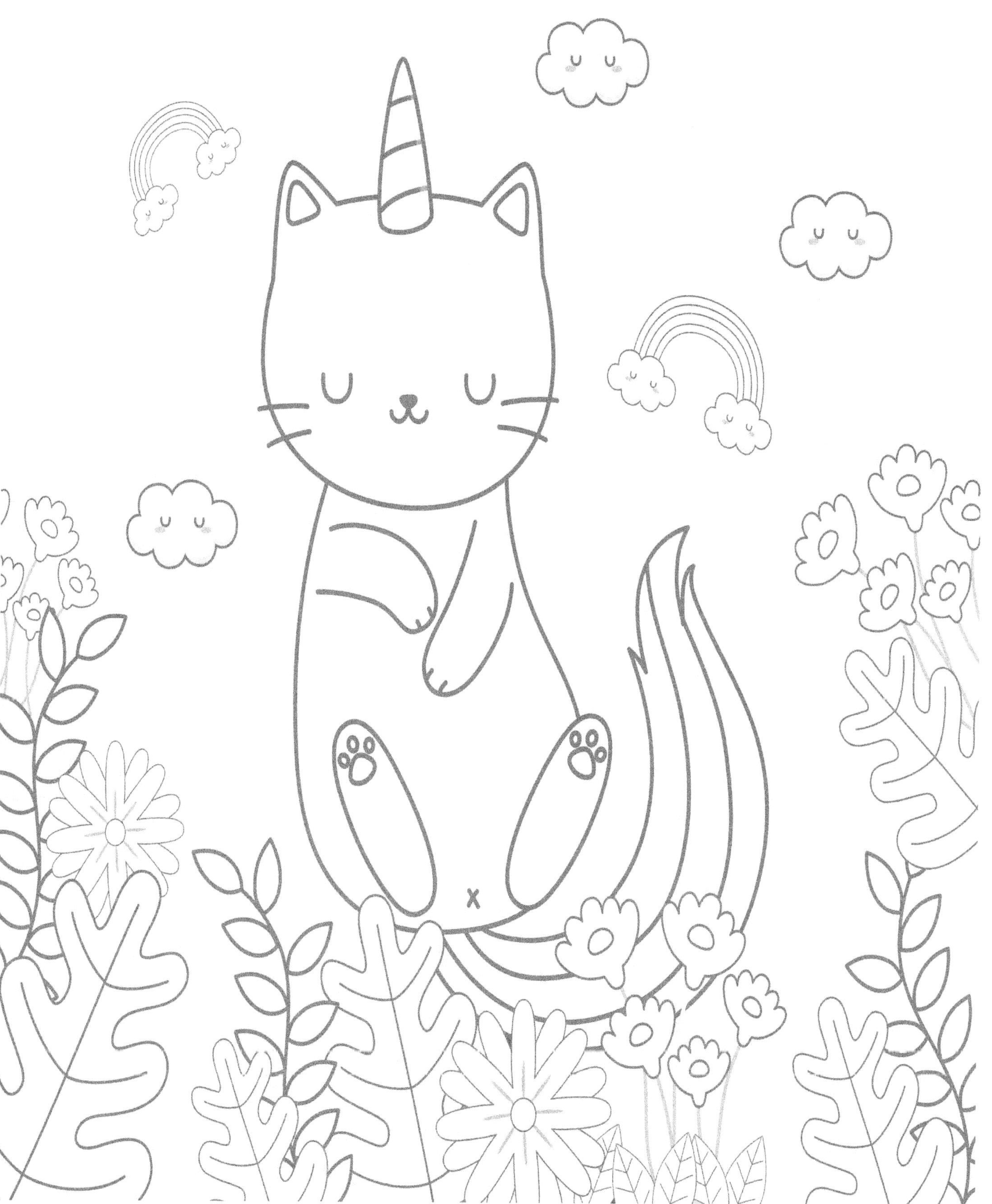

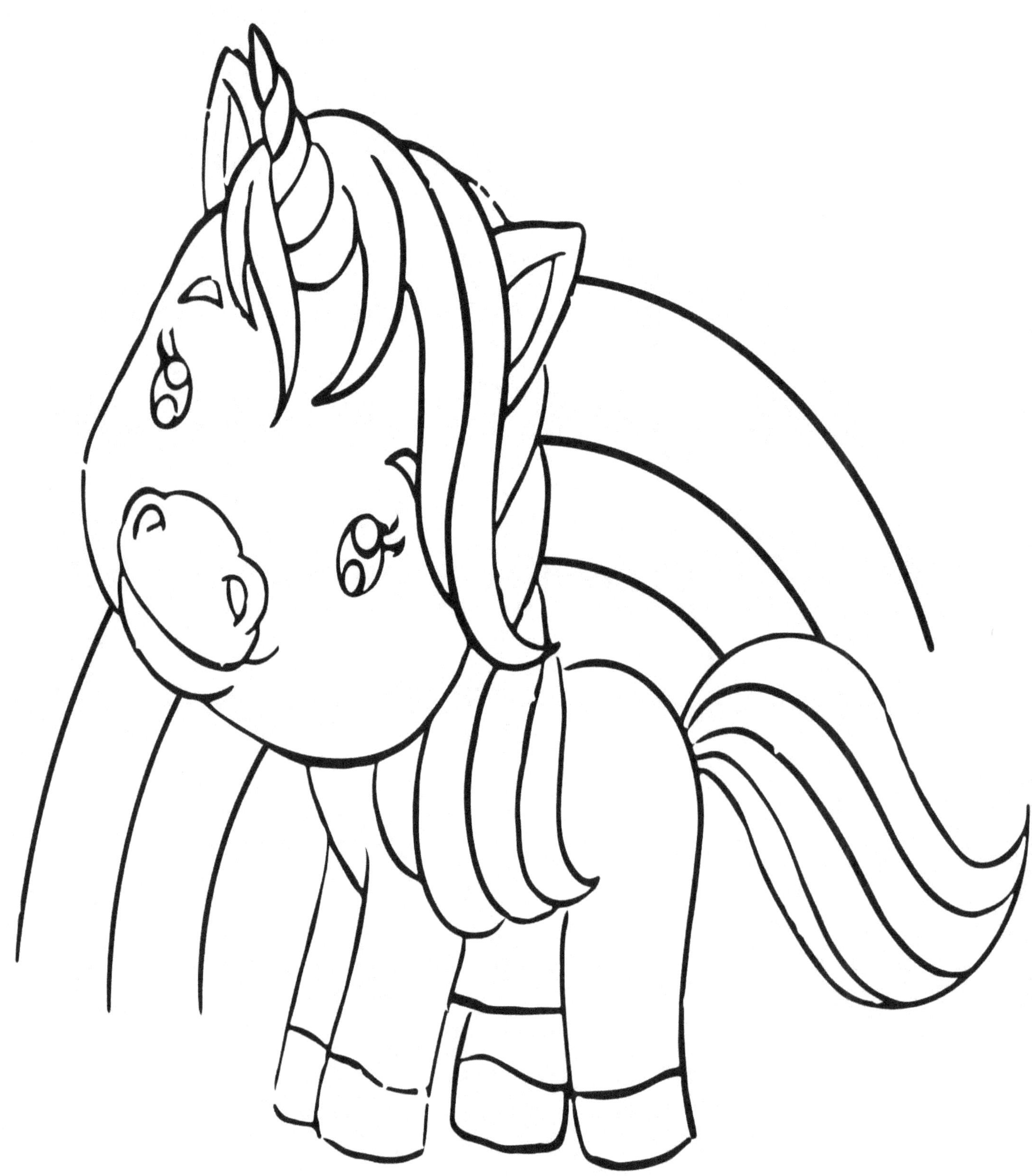

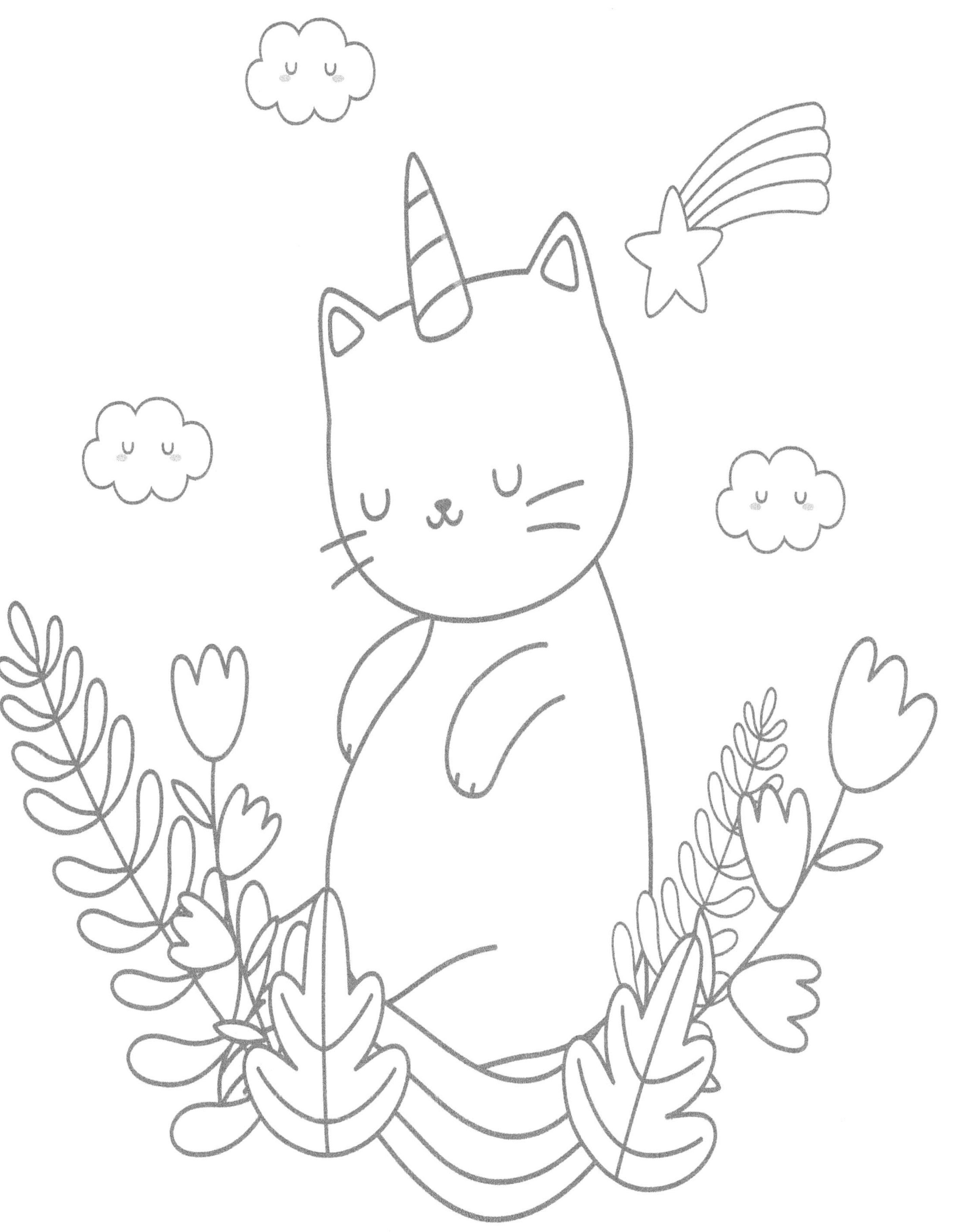

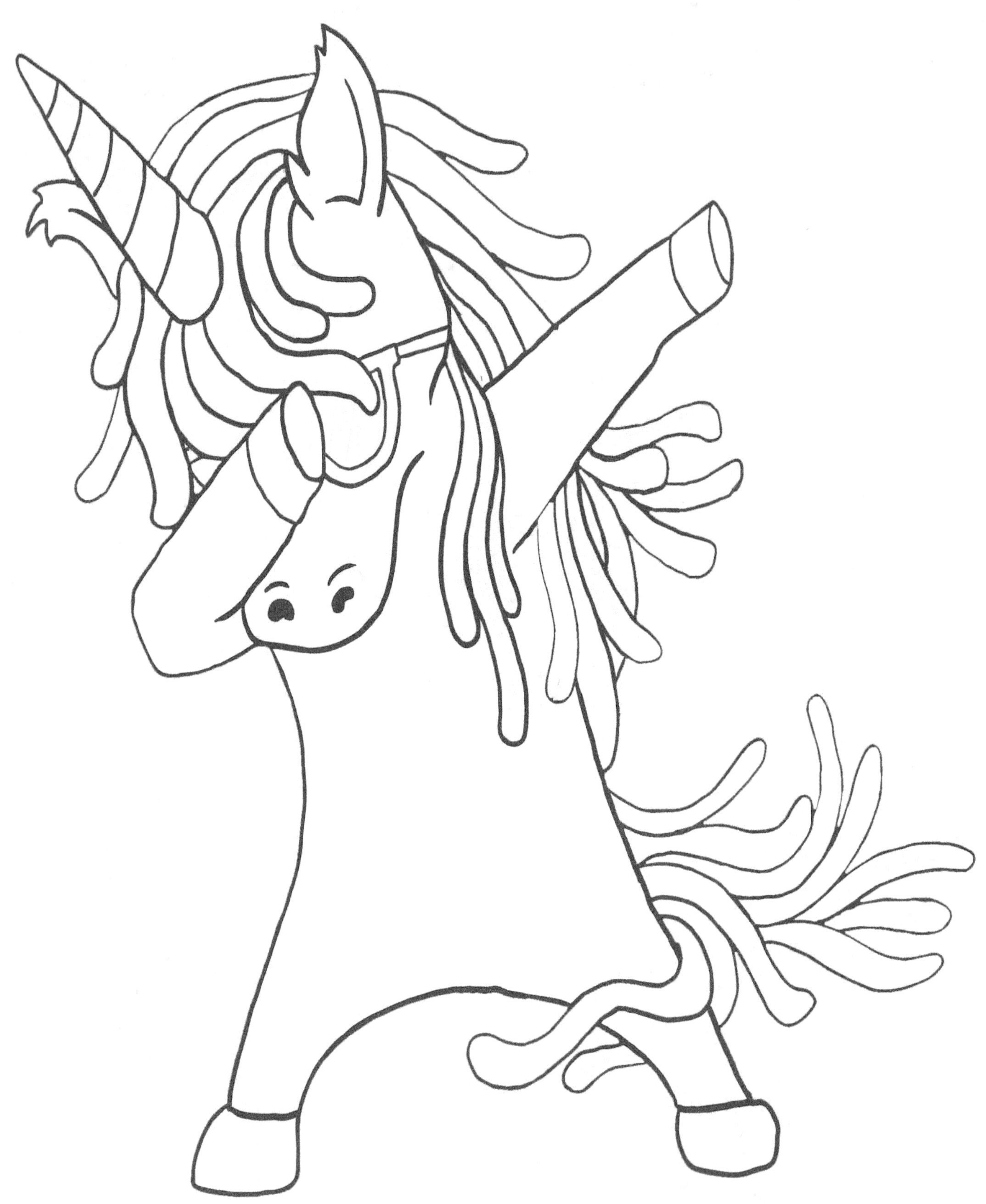

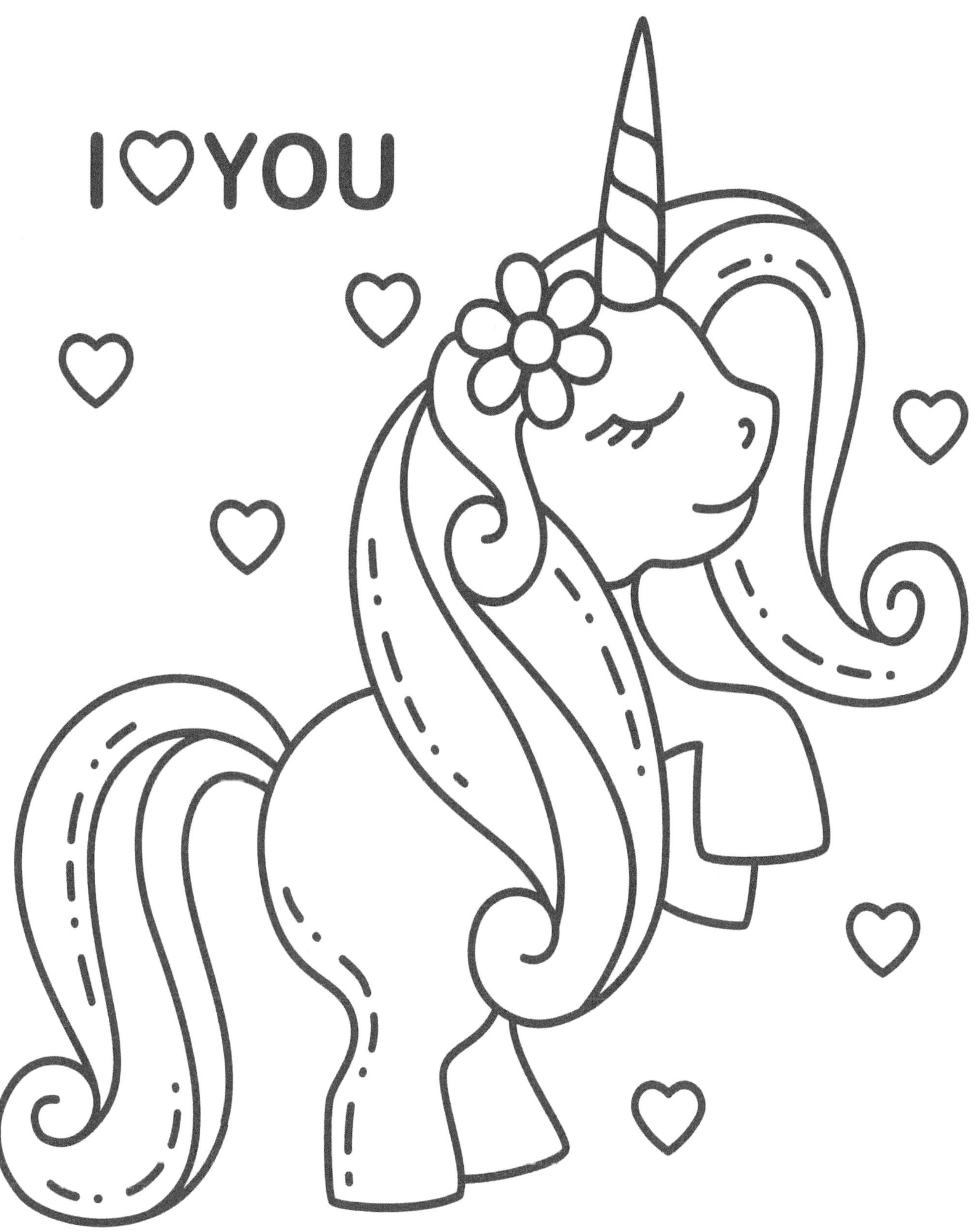

I ♥ YOU

UNICORN

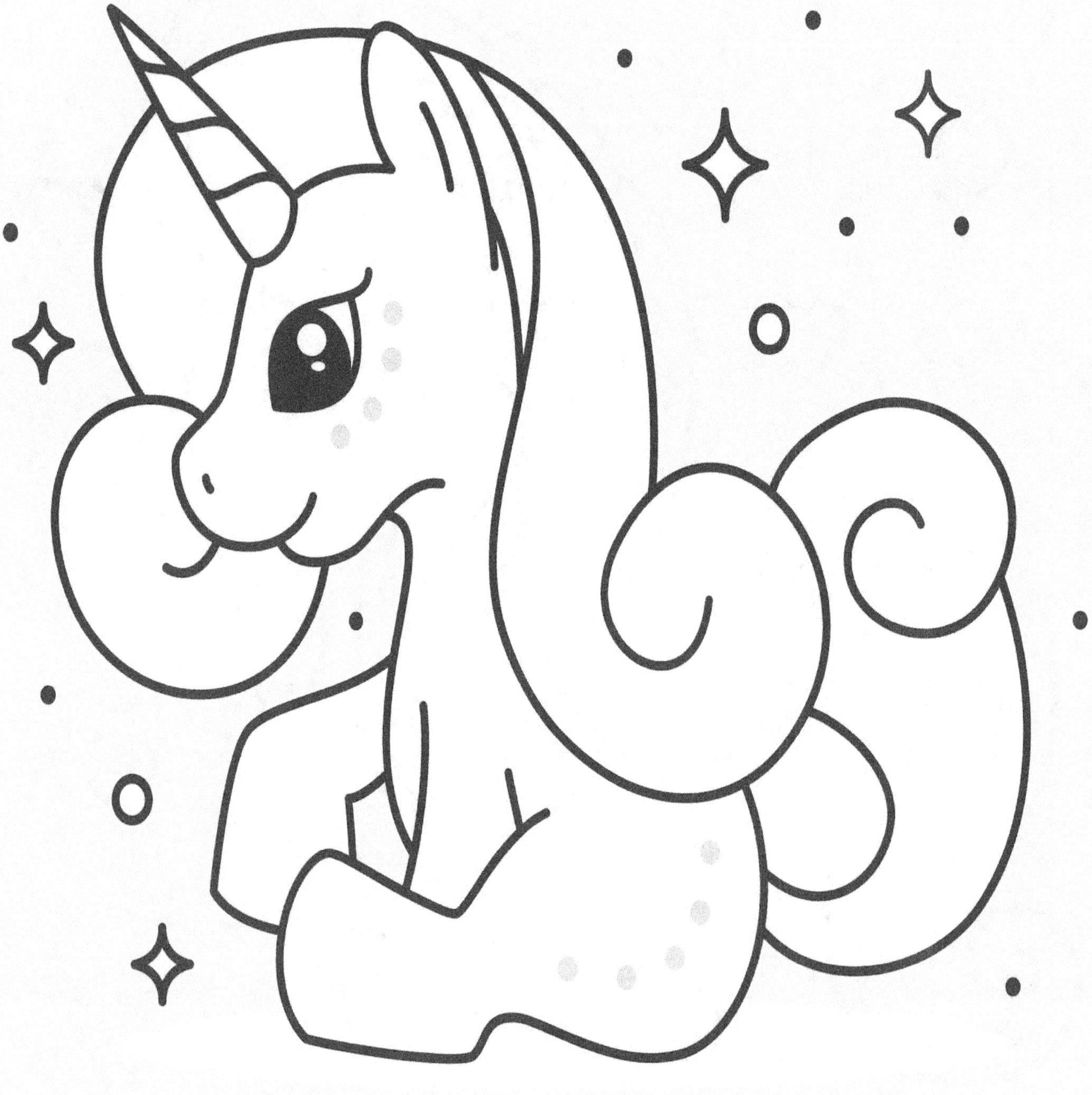

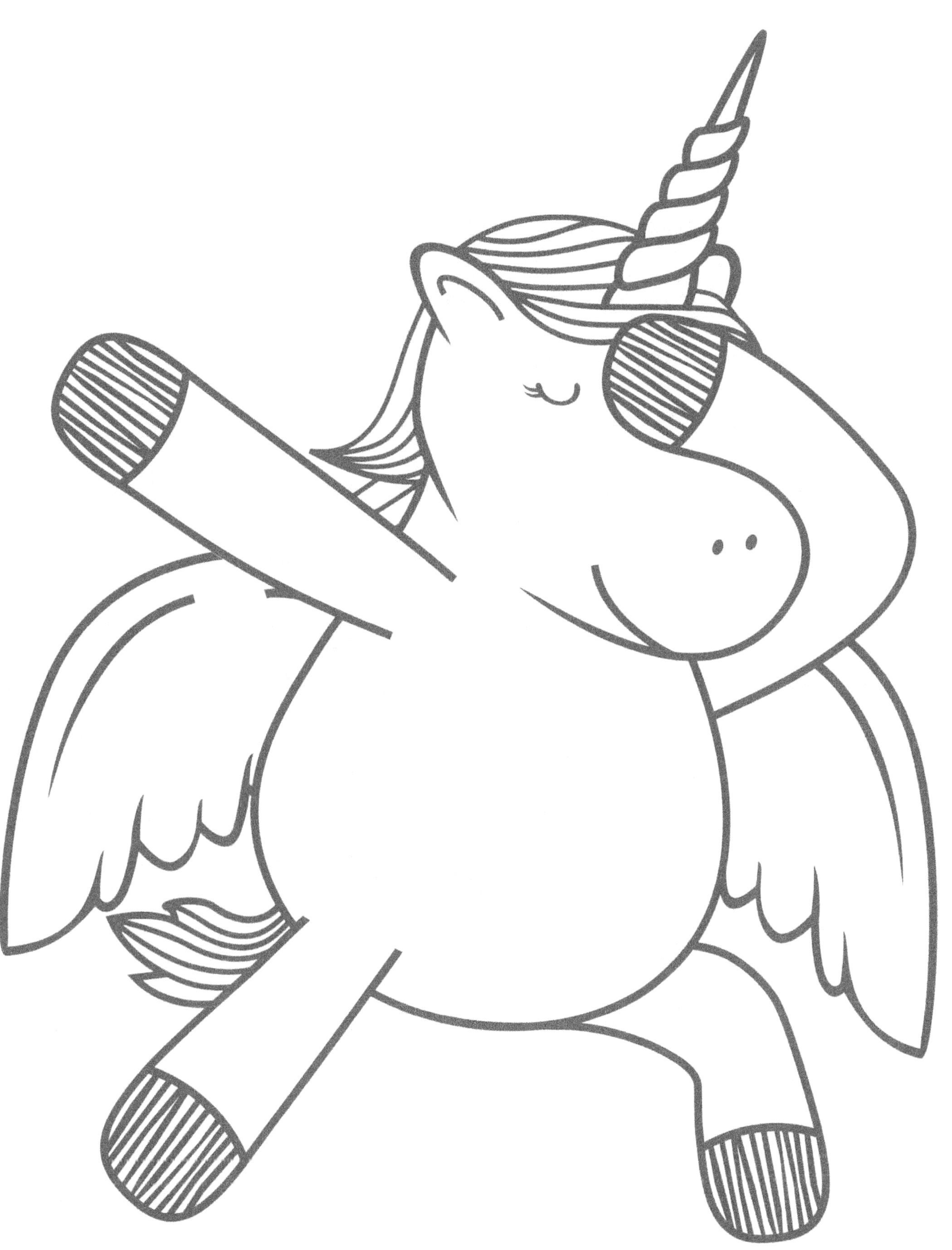

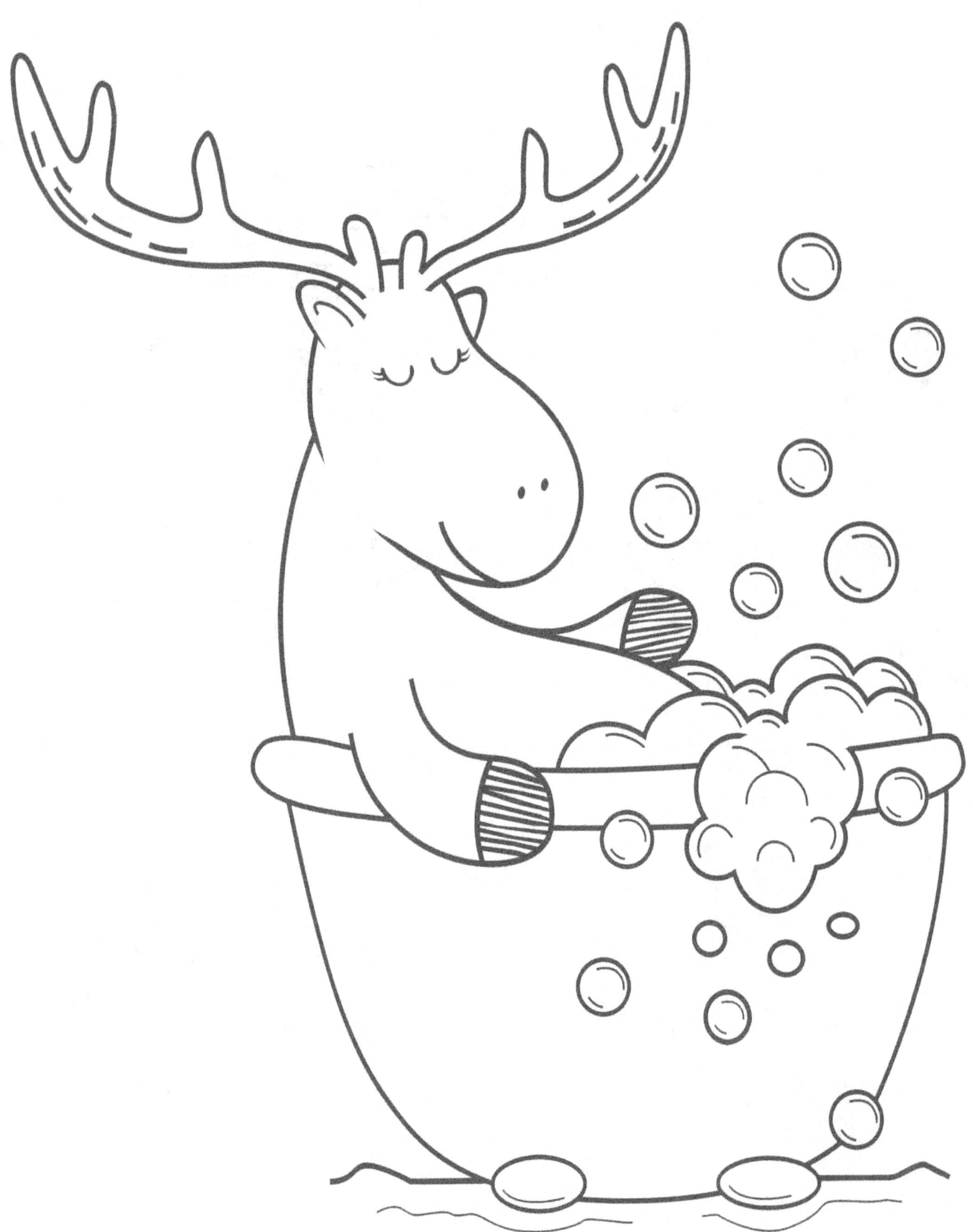

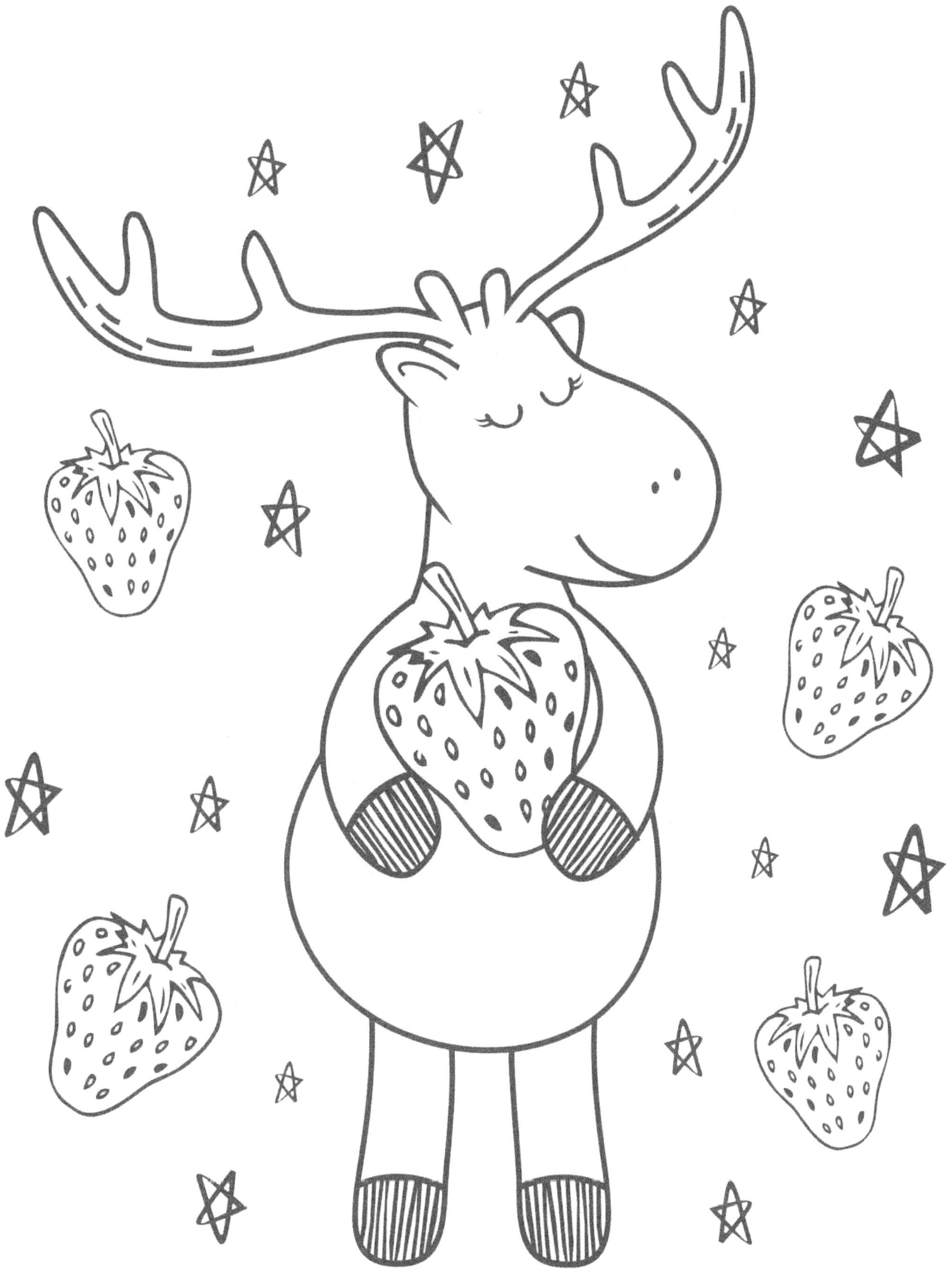

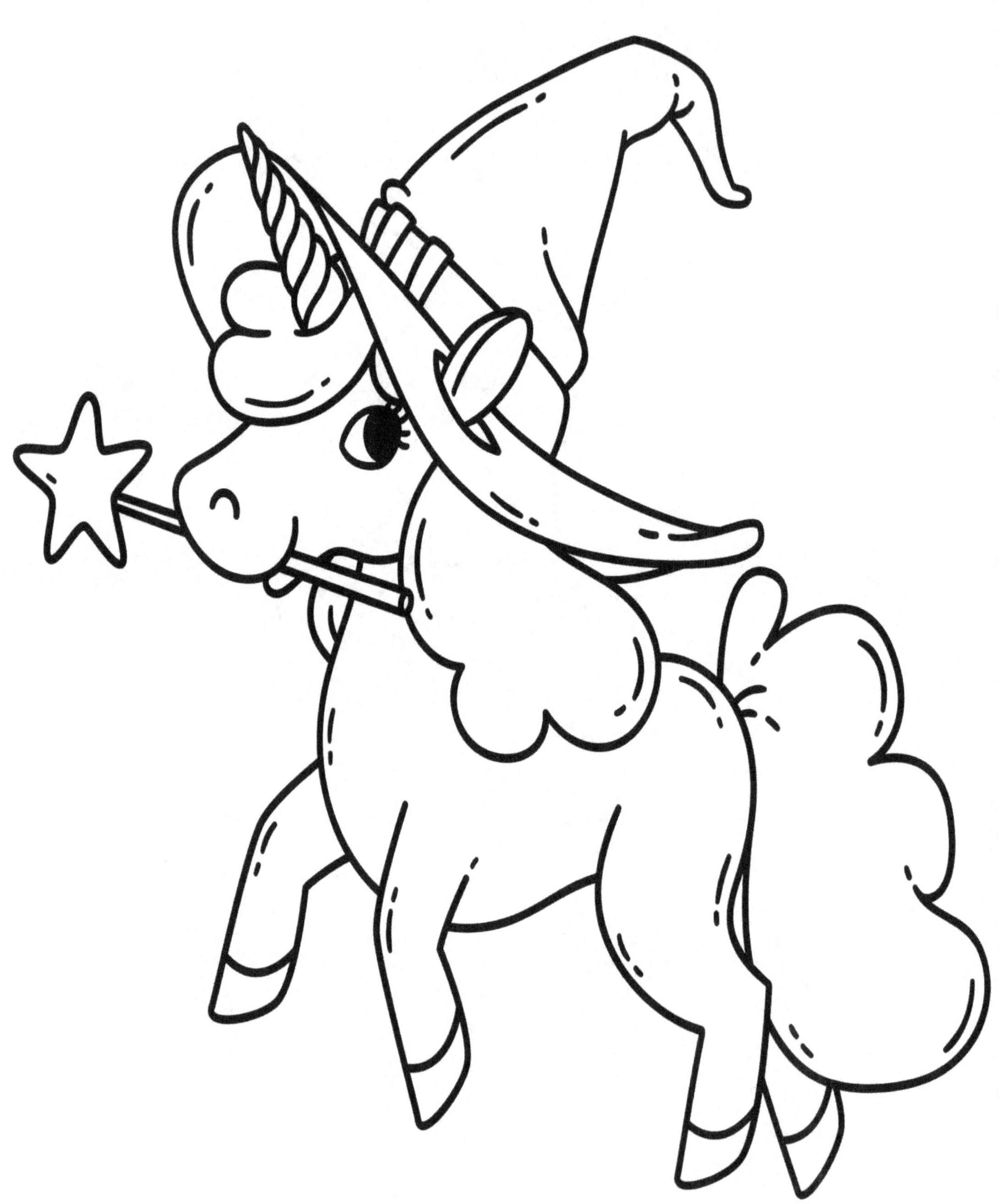

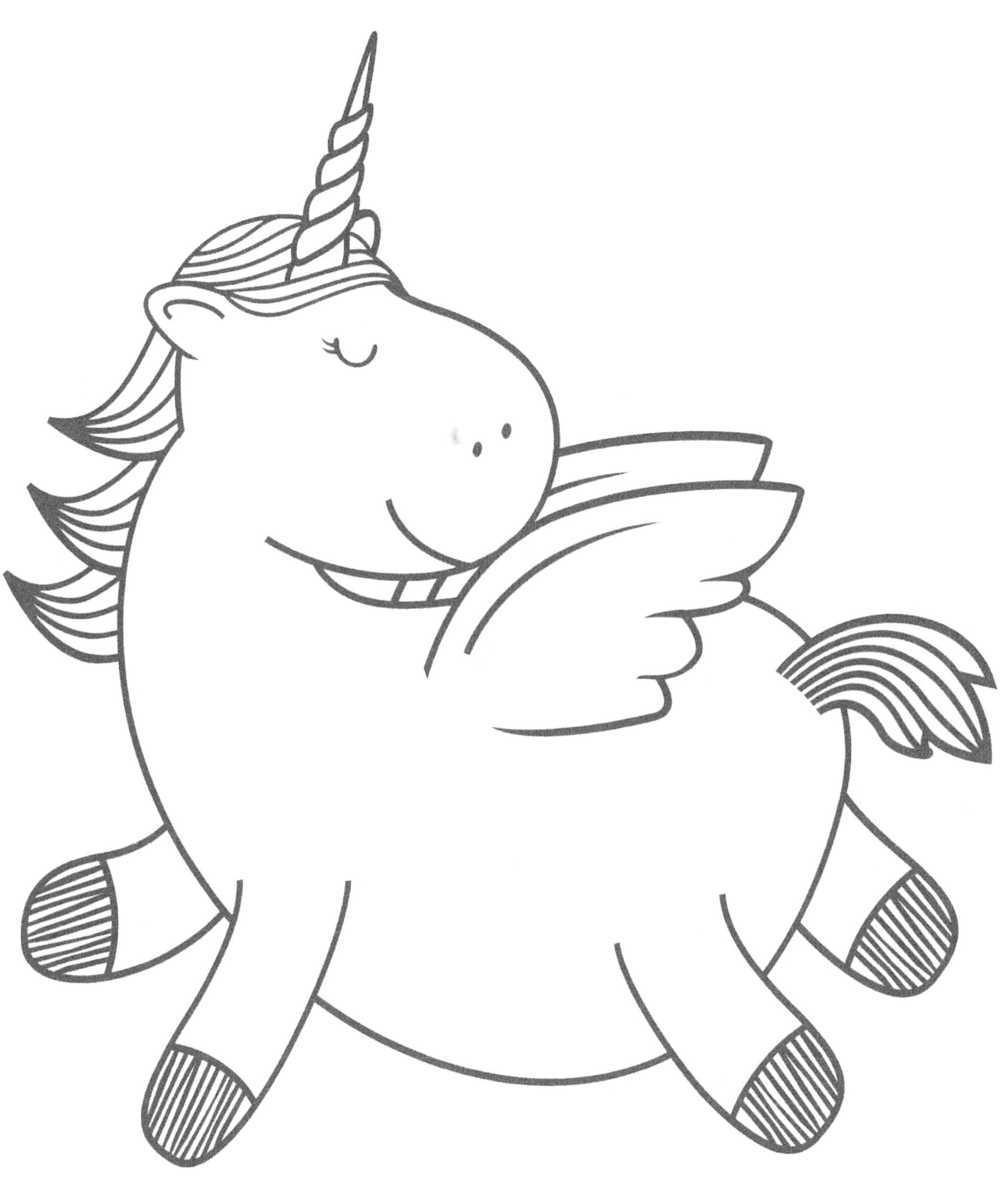

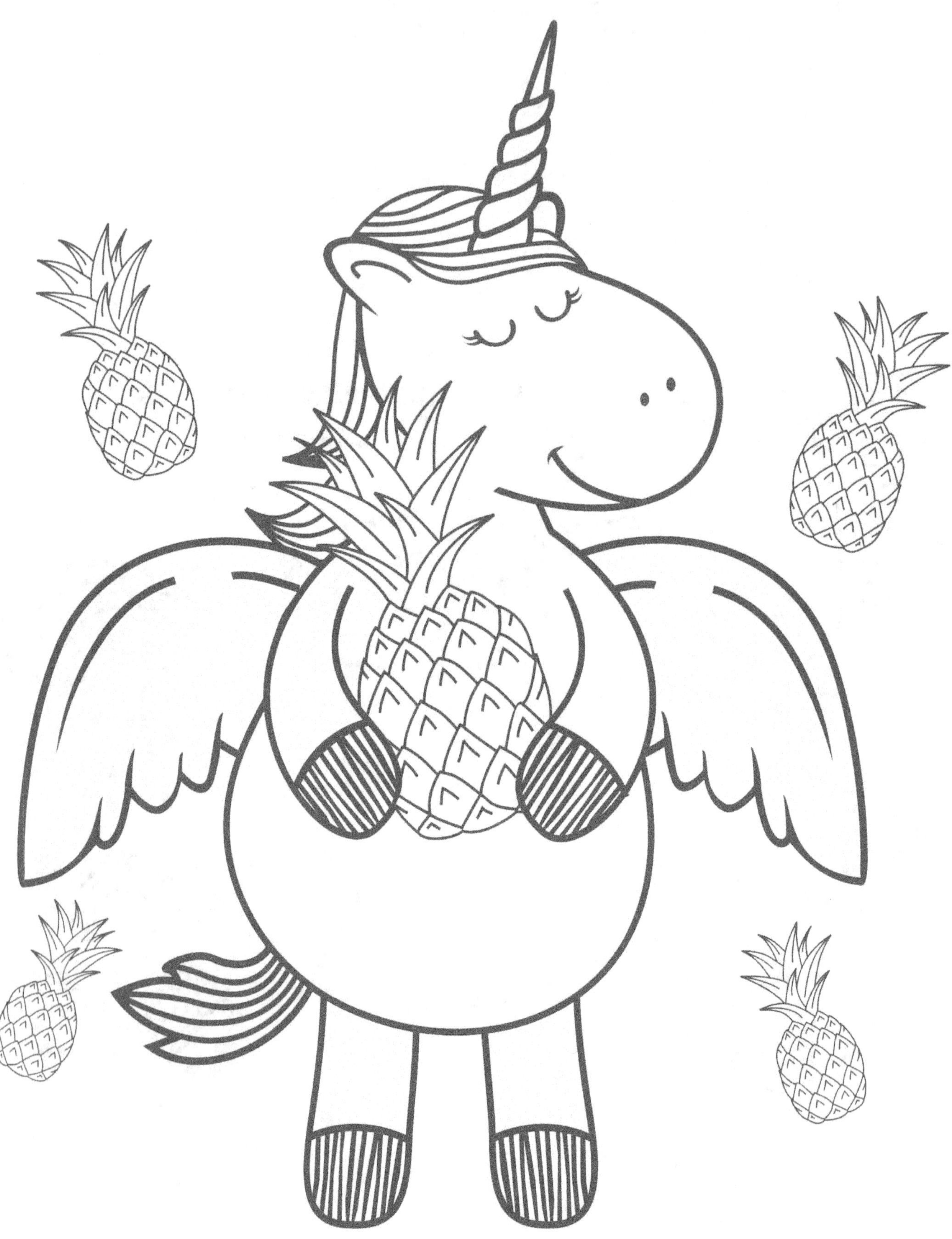

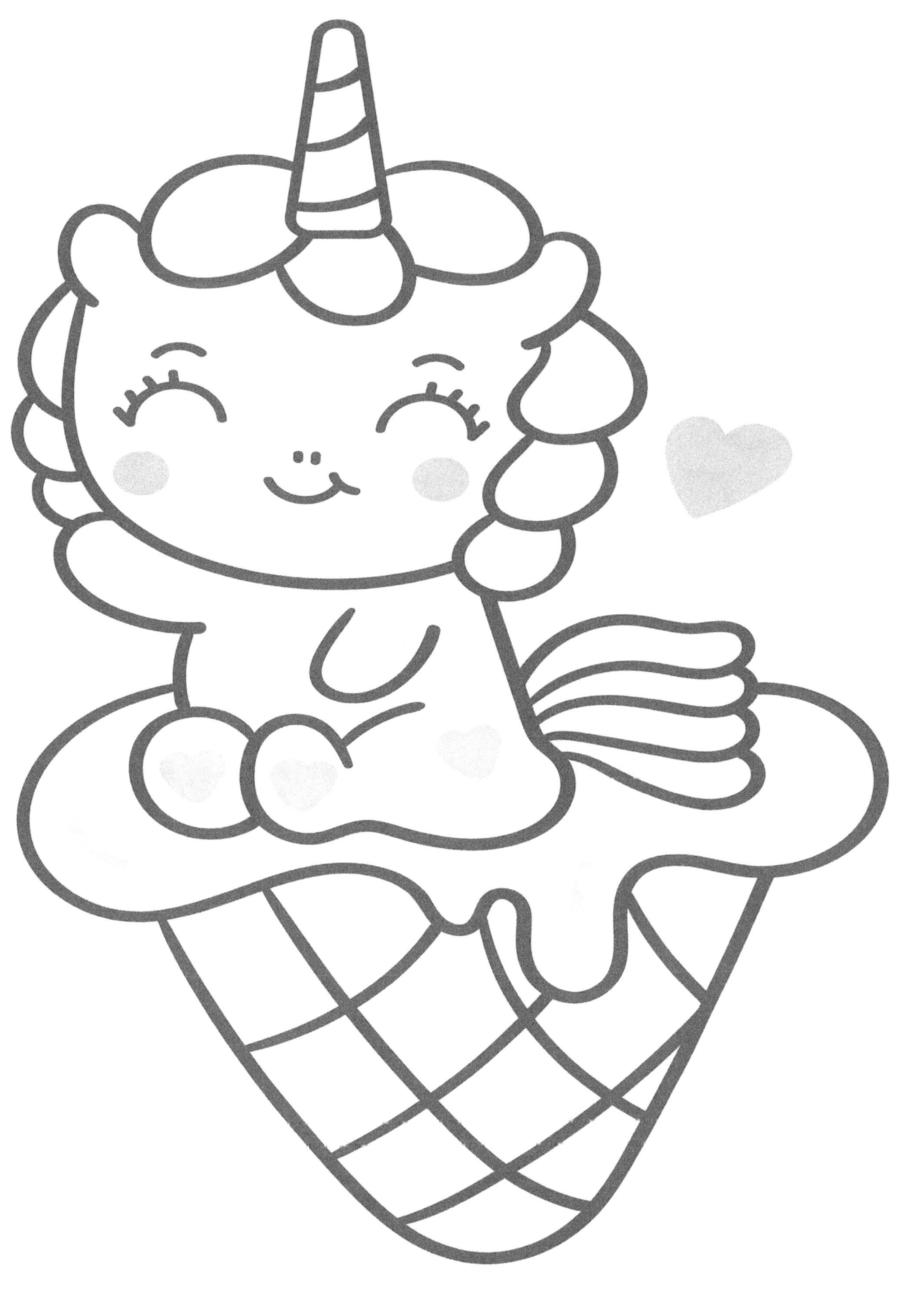

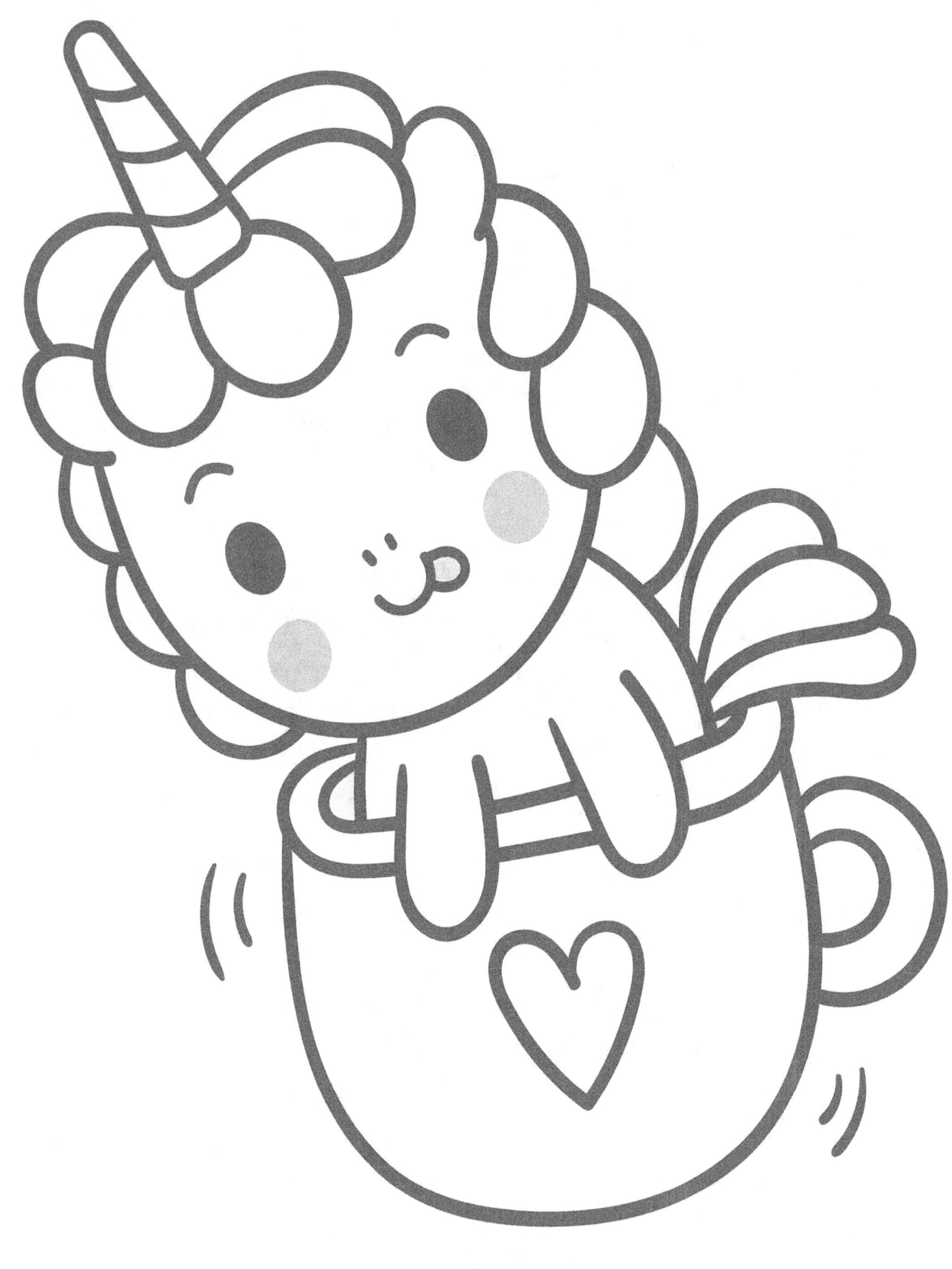

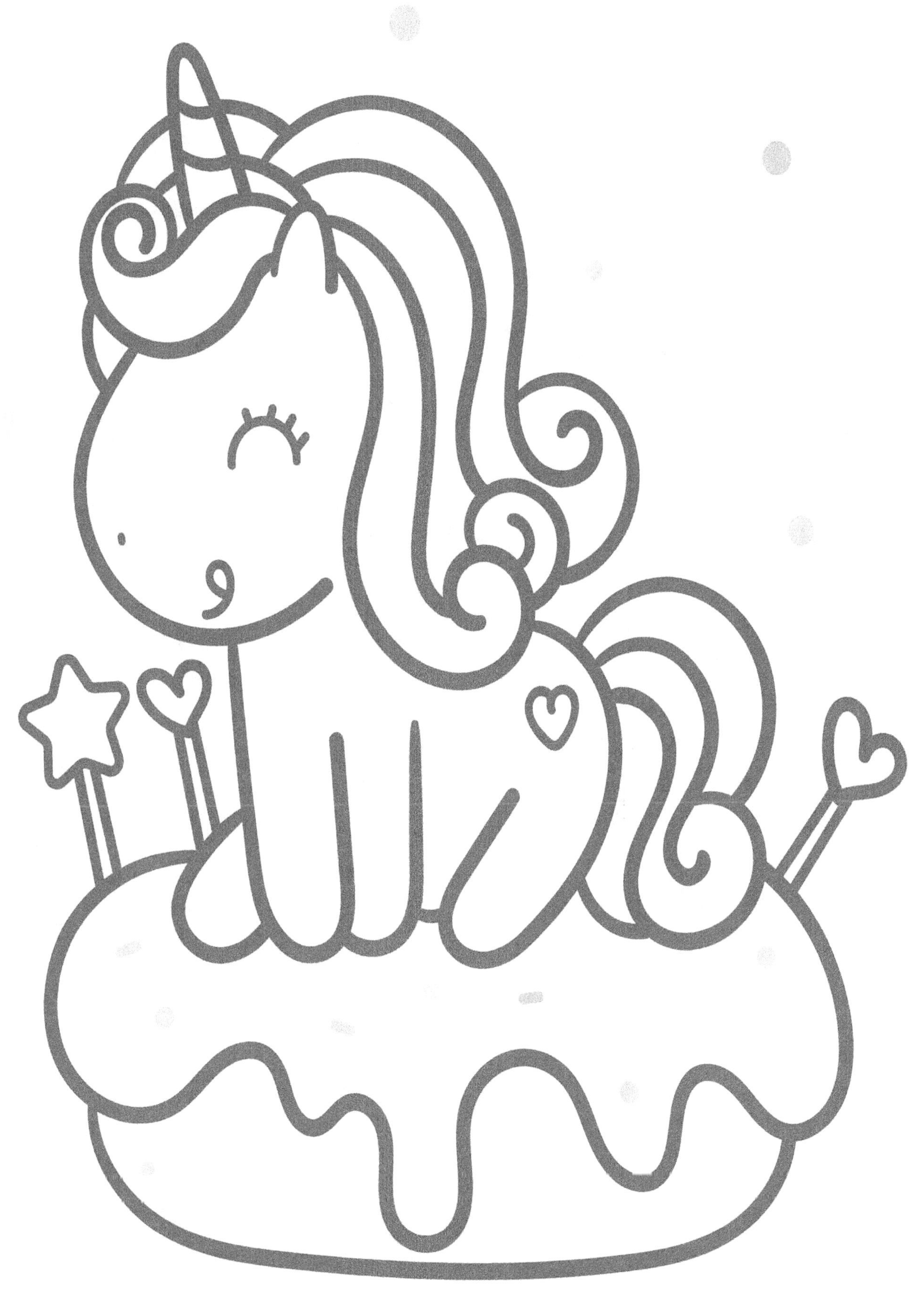

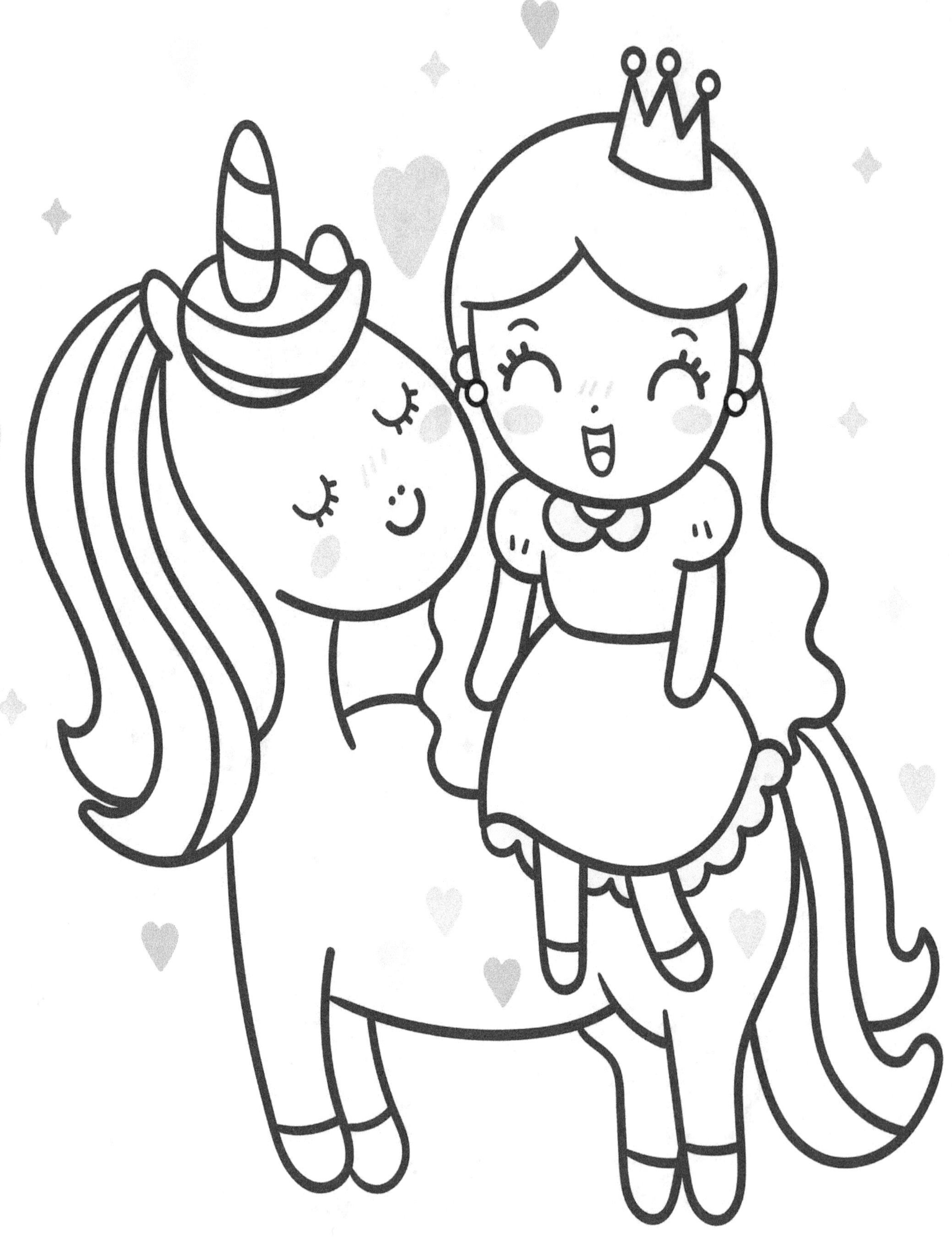

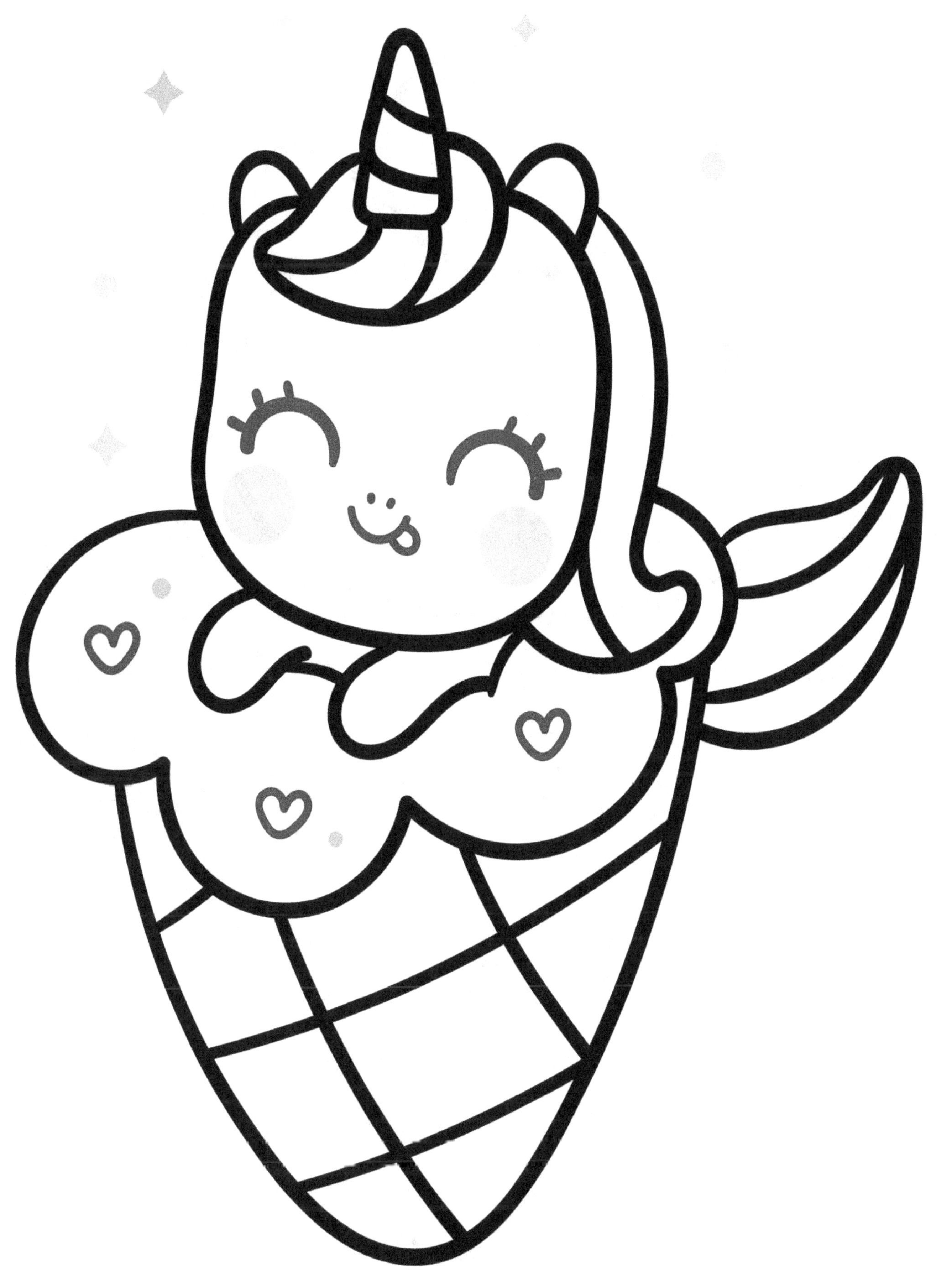

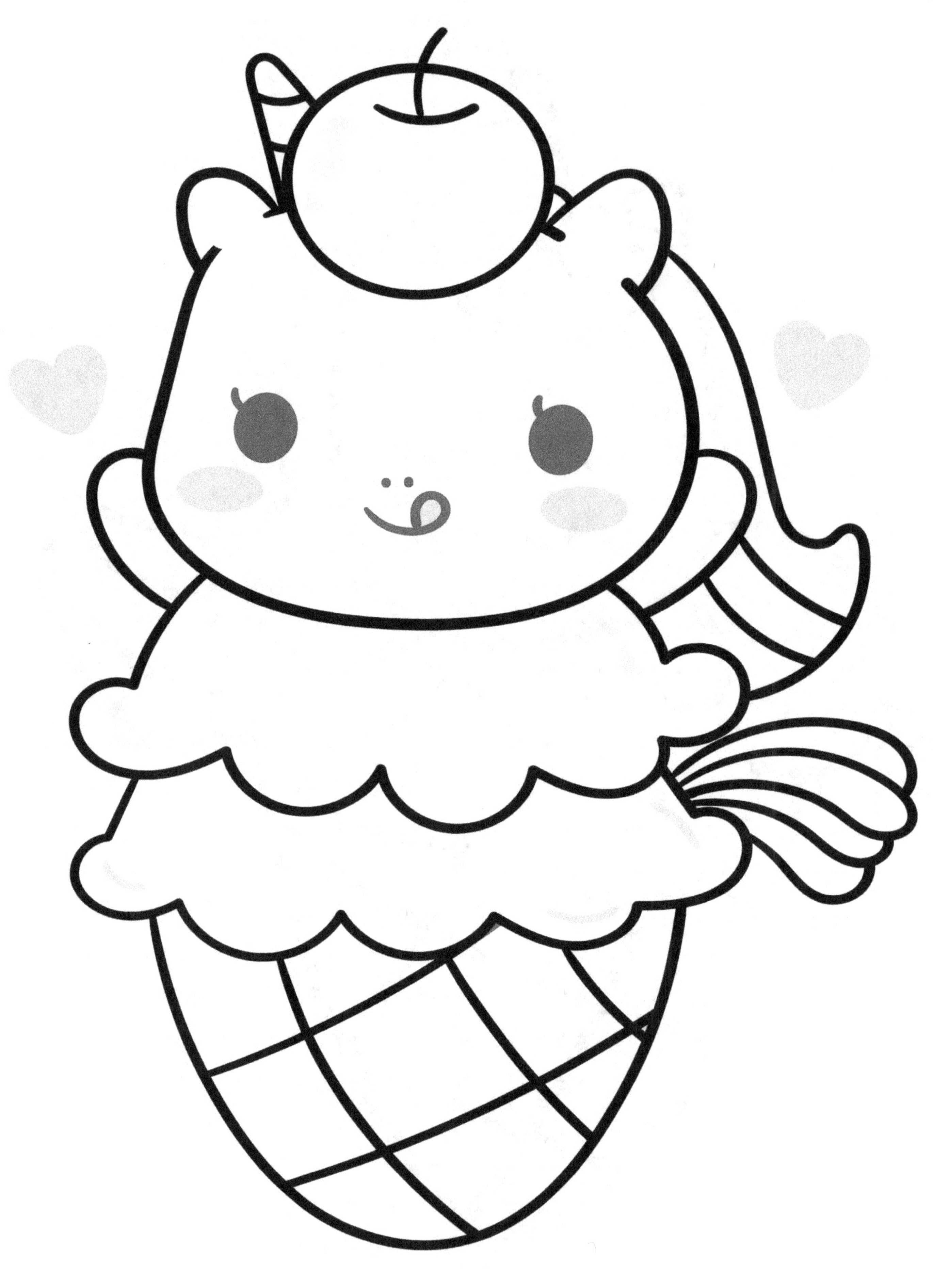

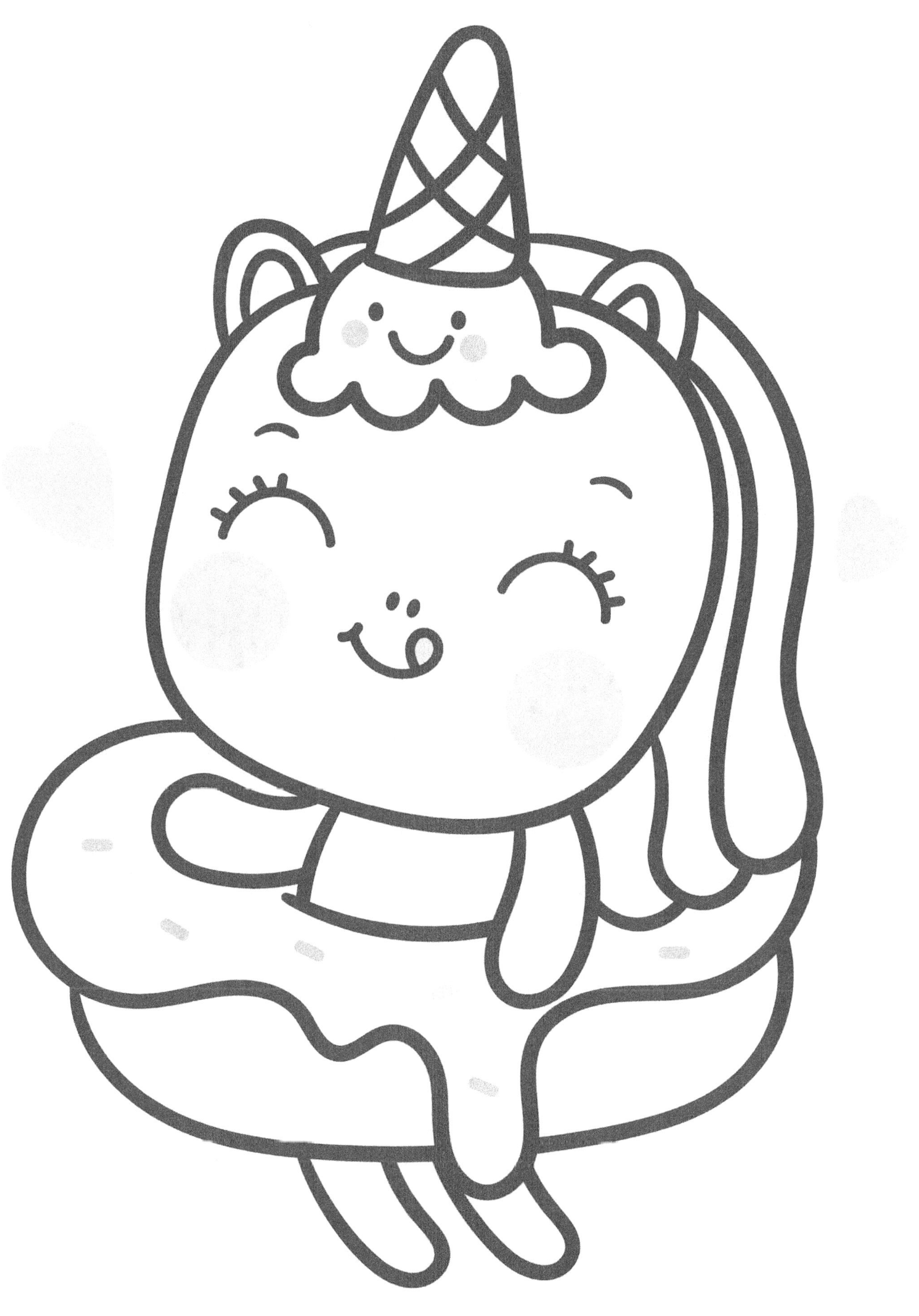

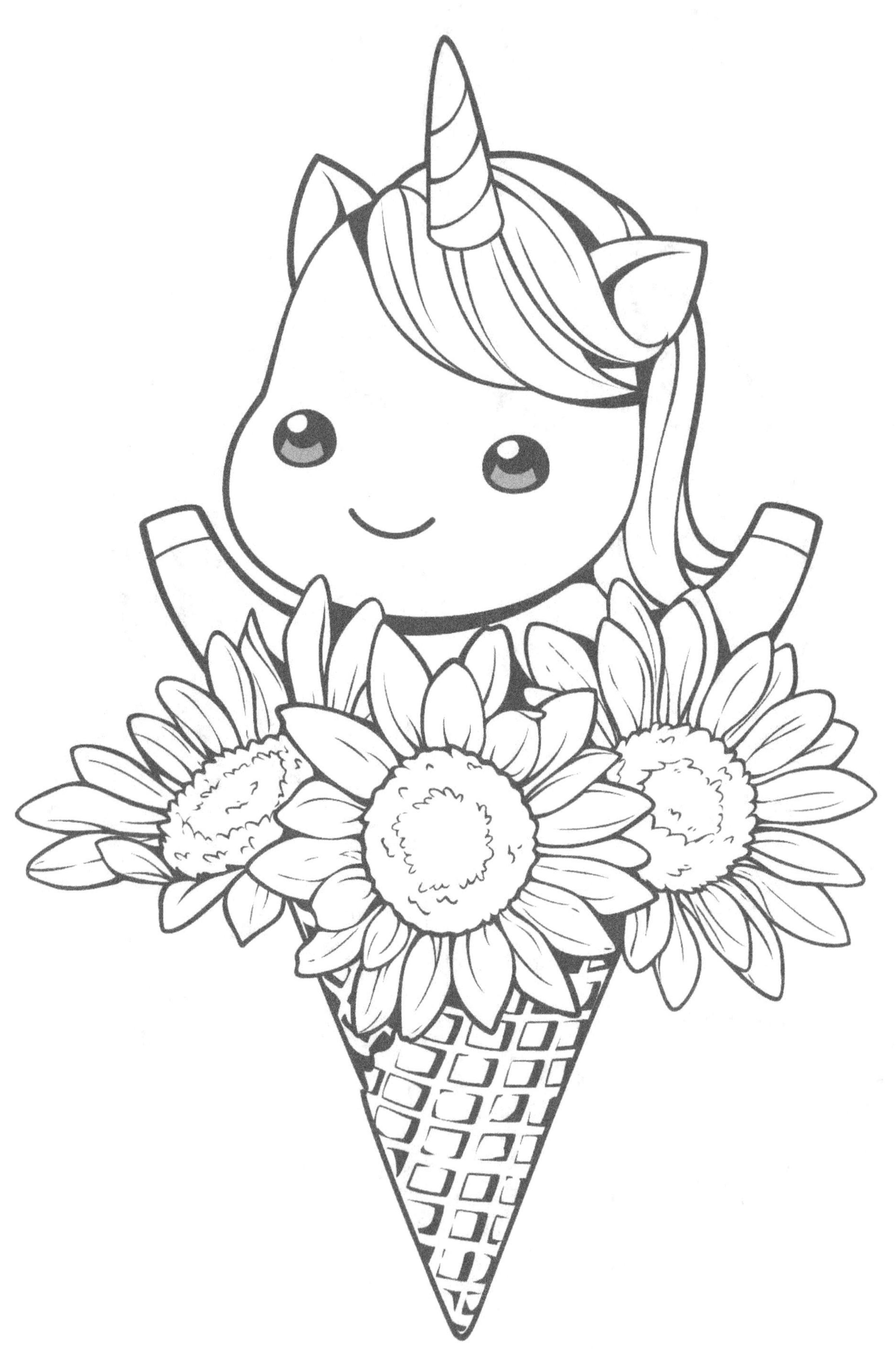

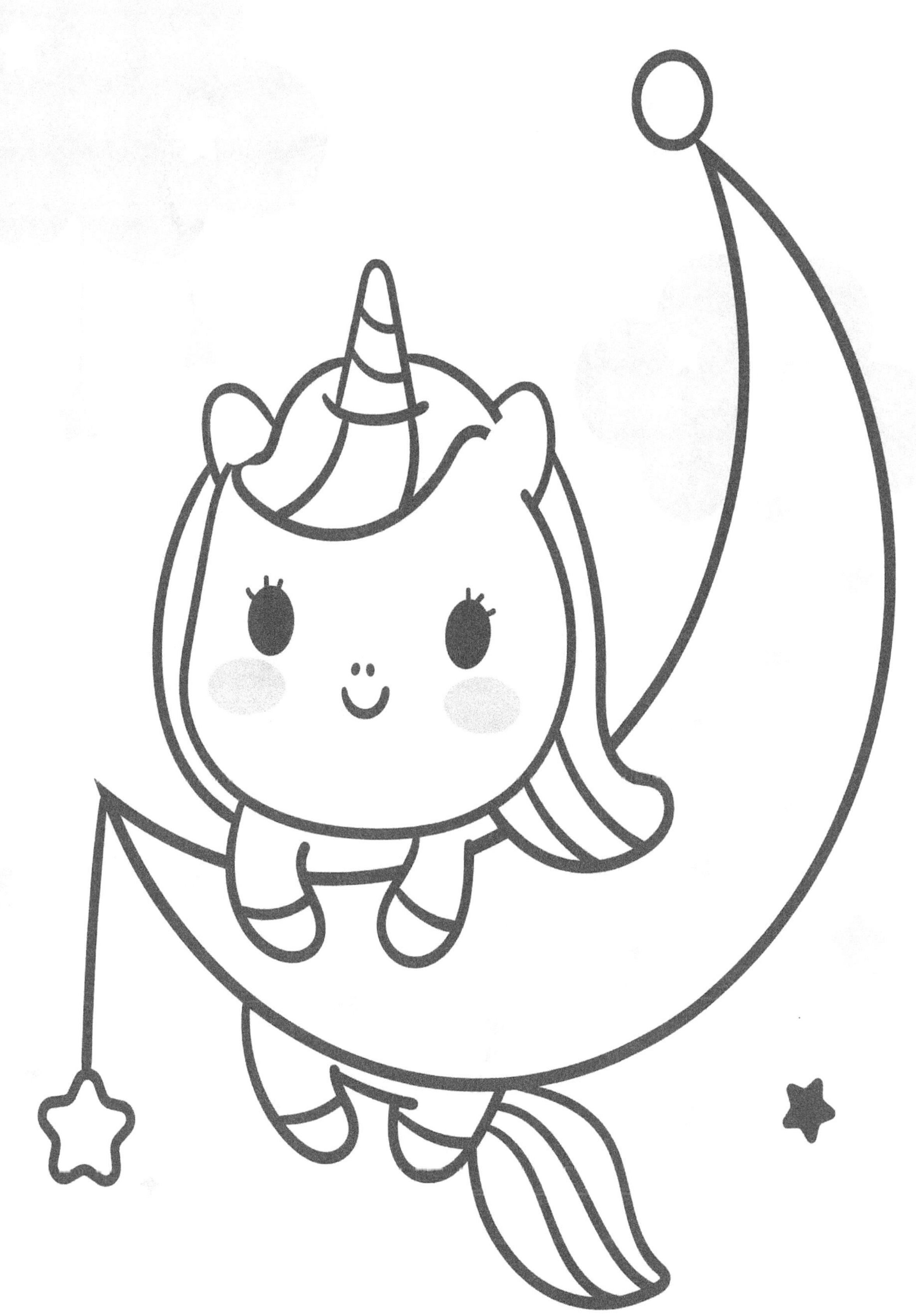

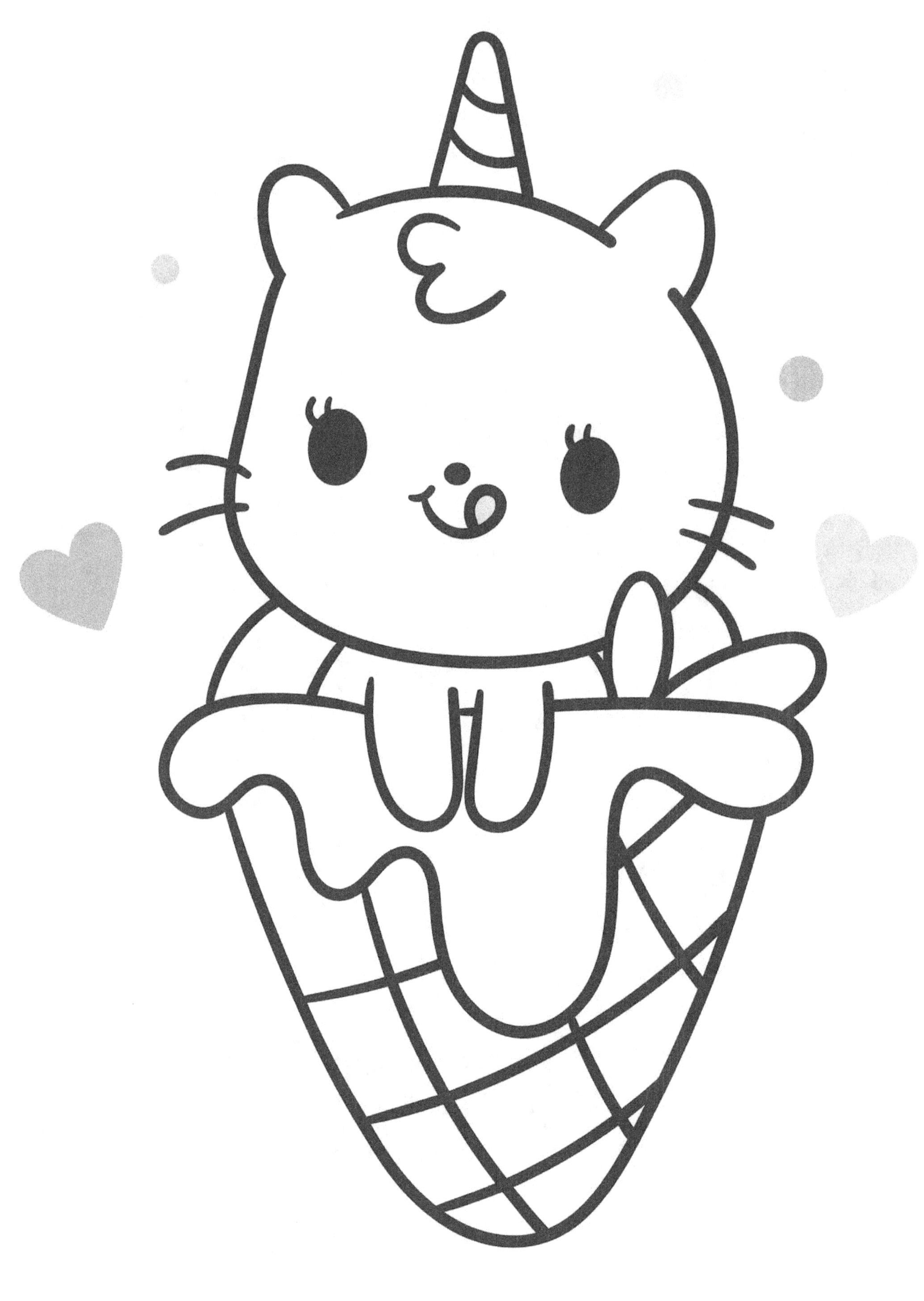

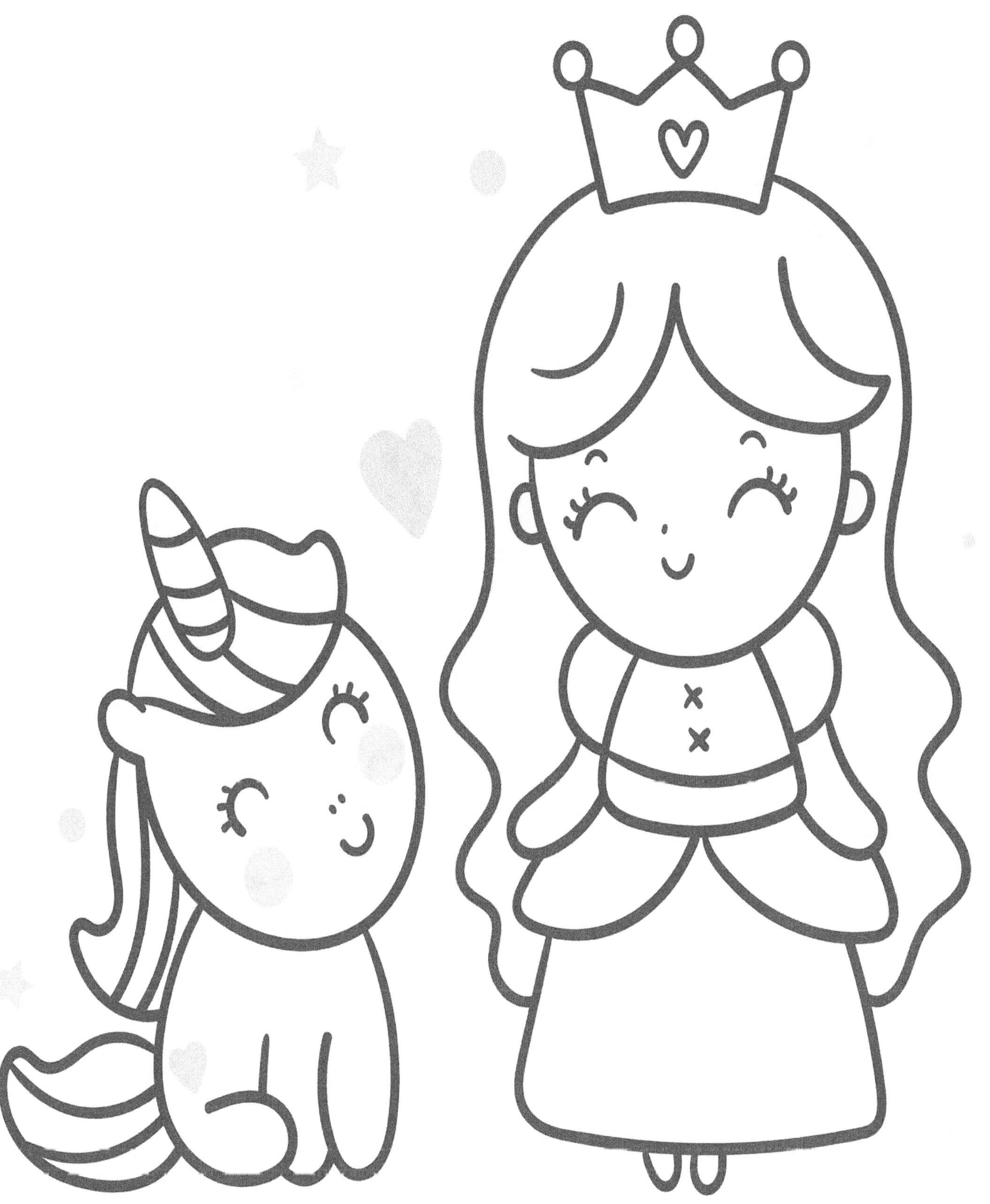

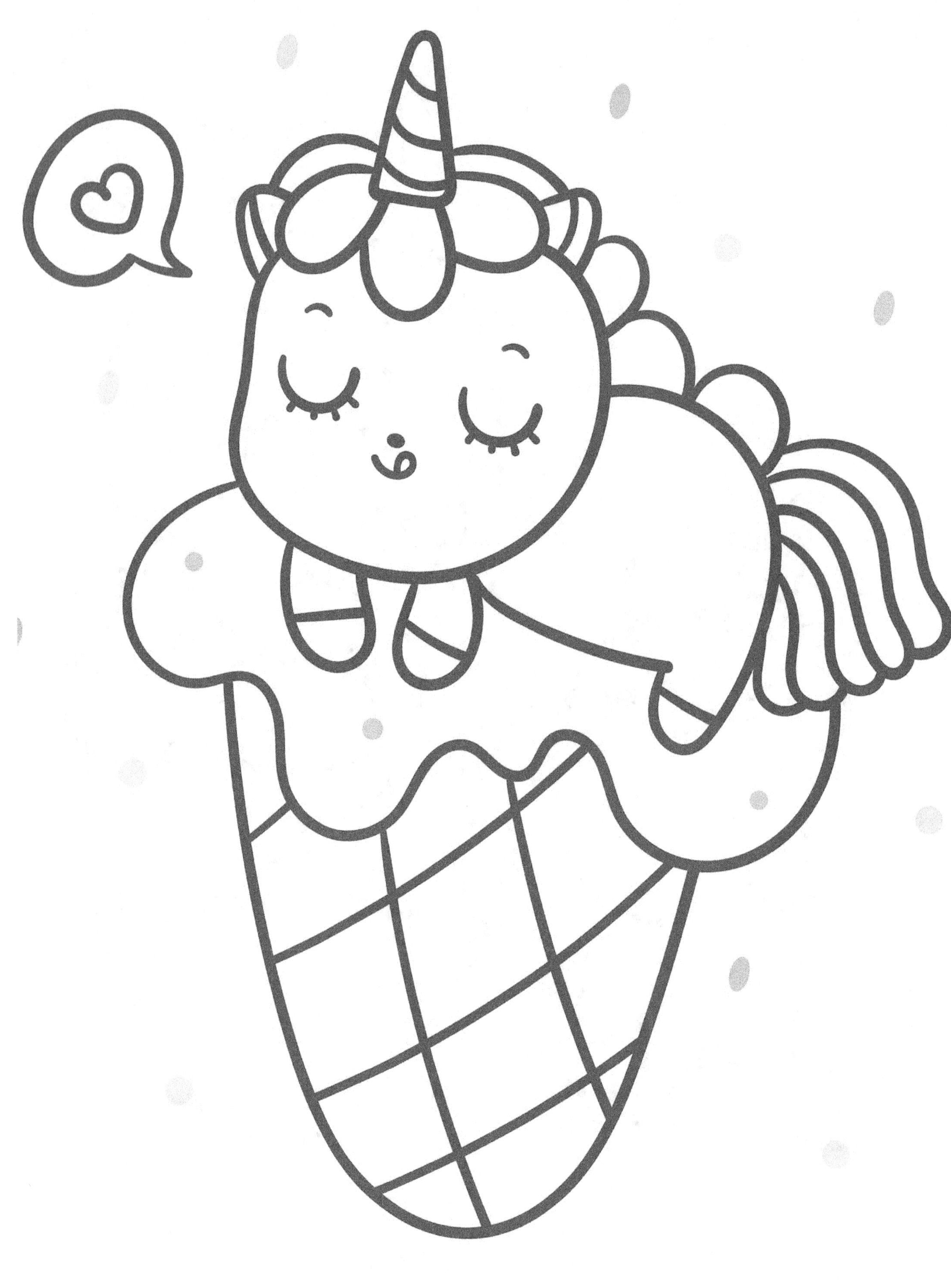

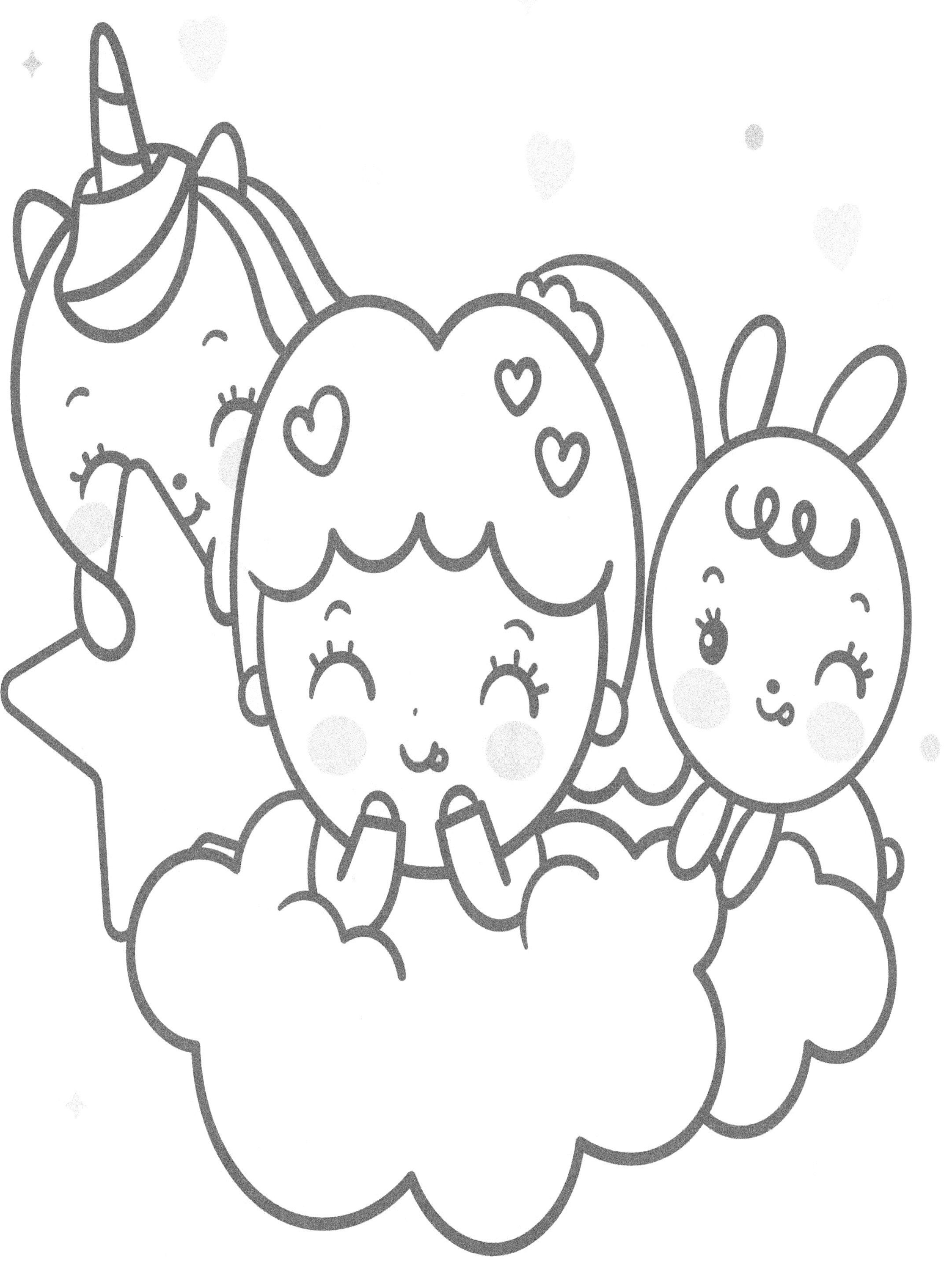

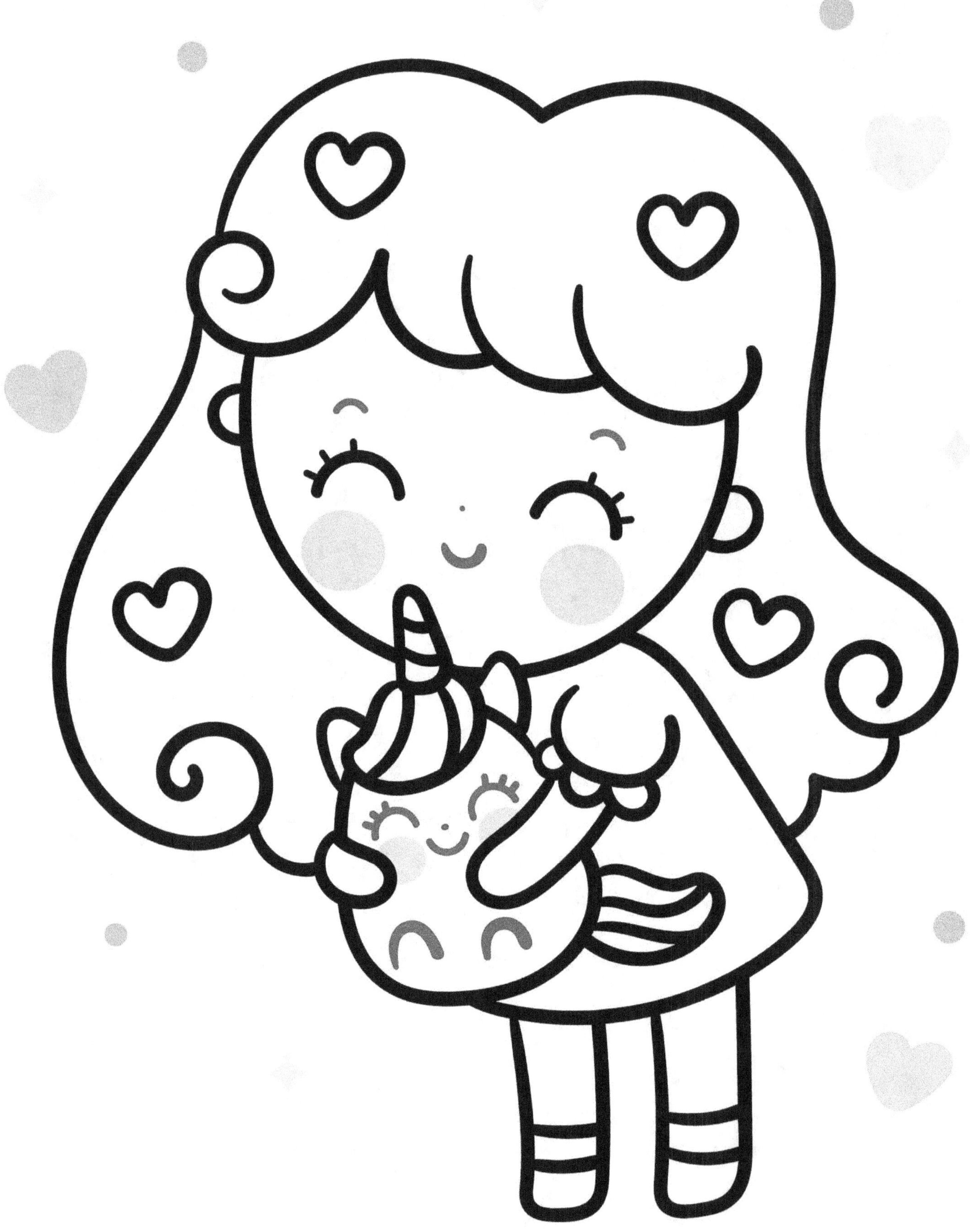

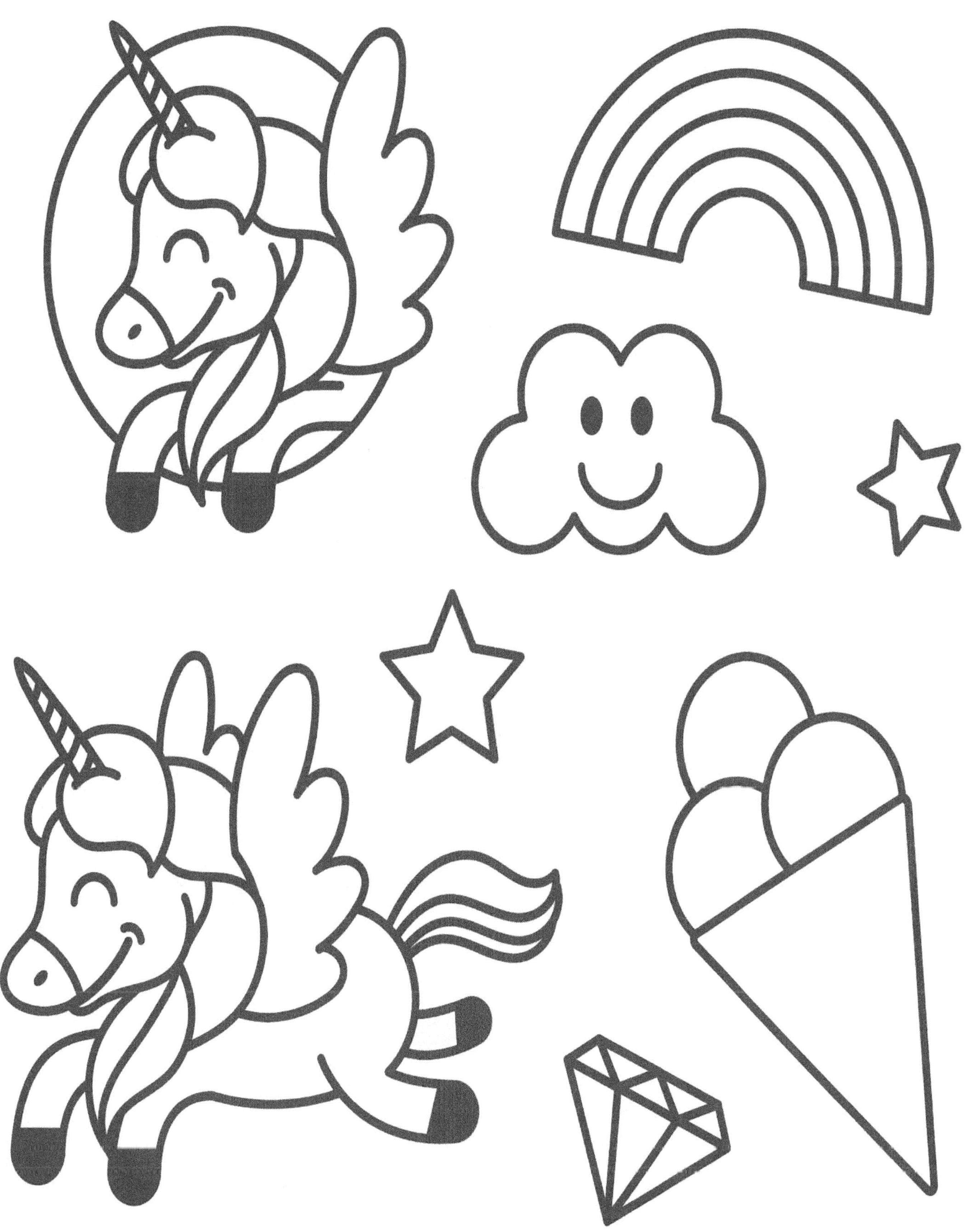

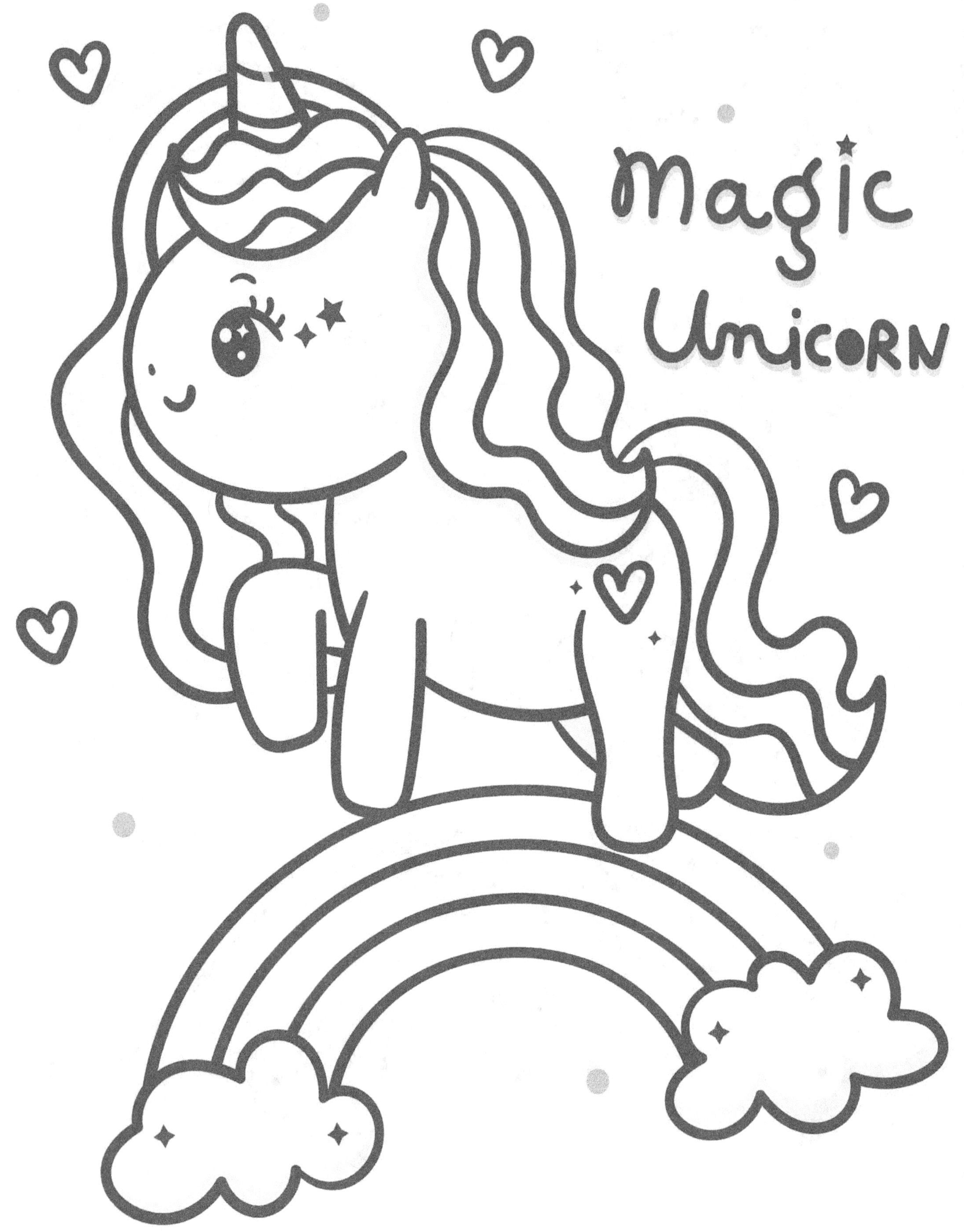

Magic
Unicorn

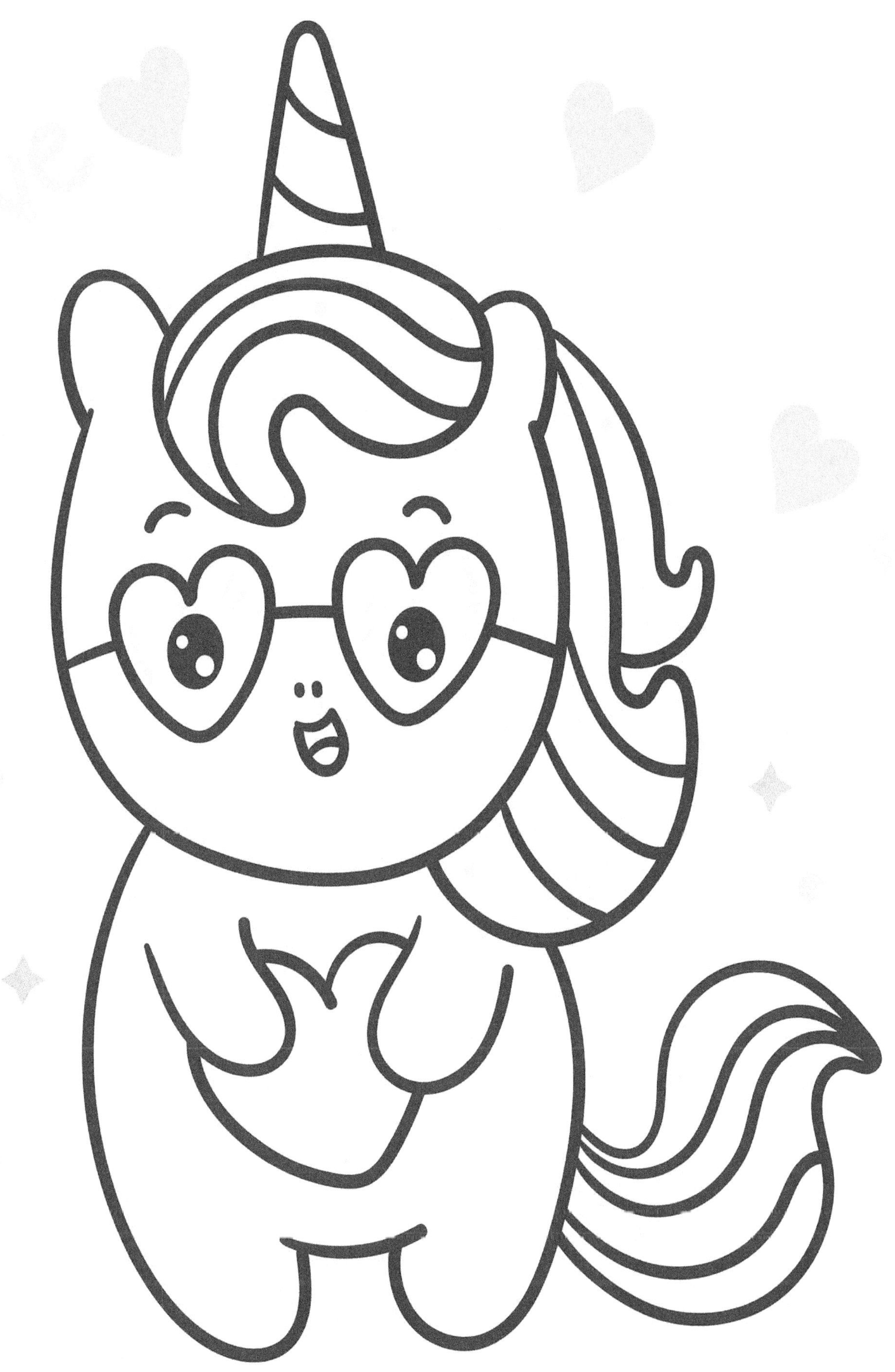
Love

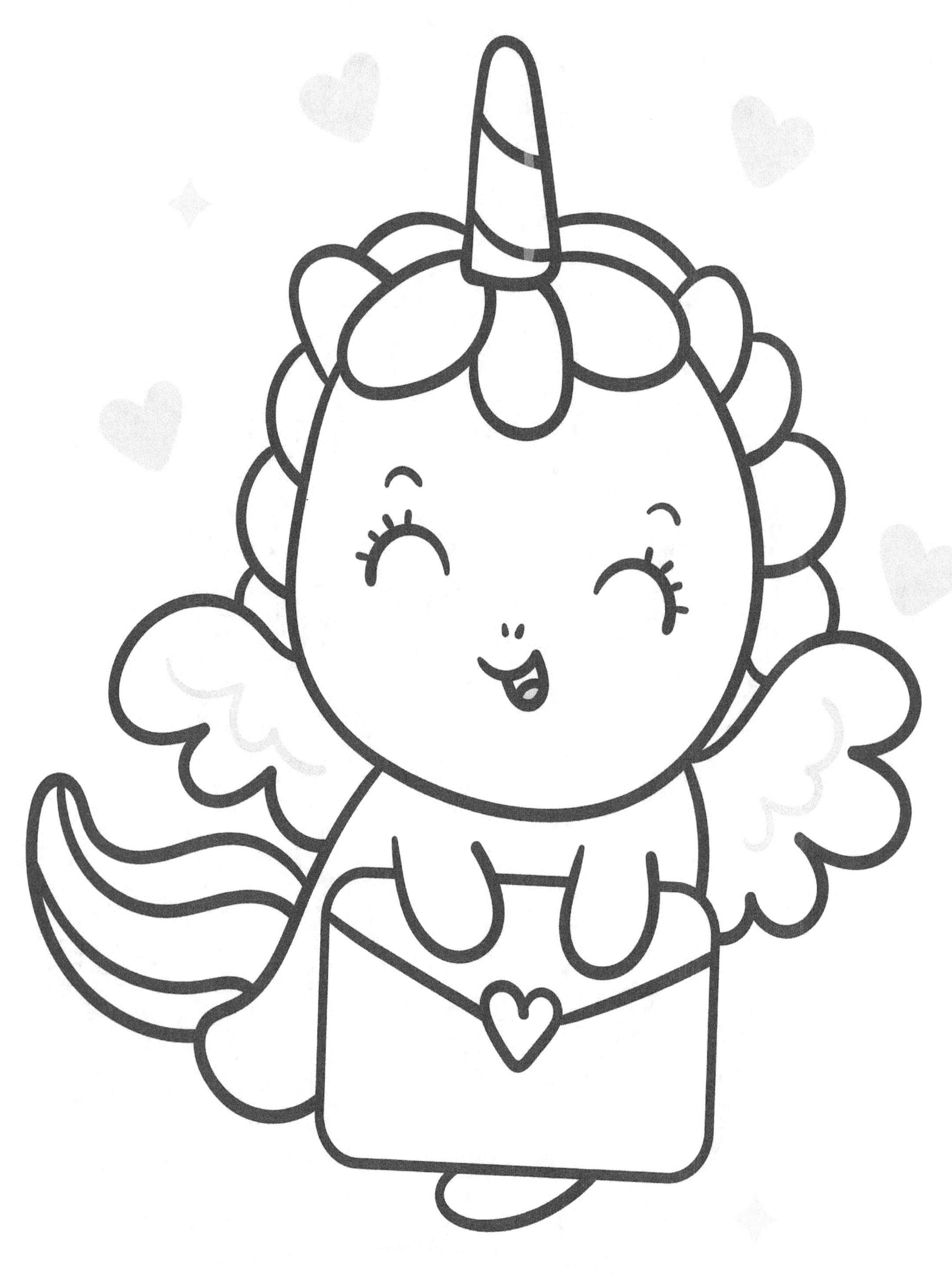

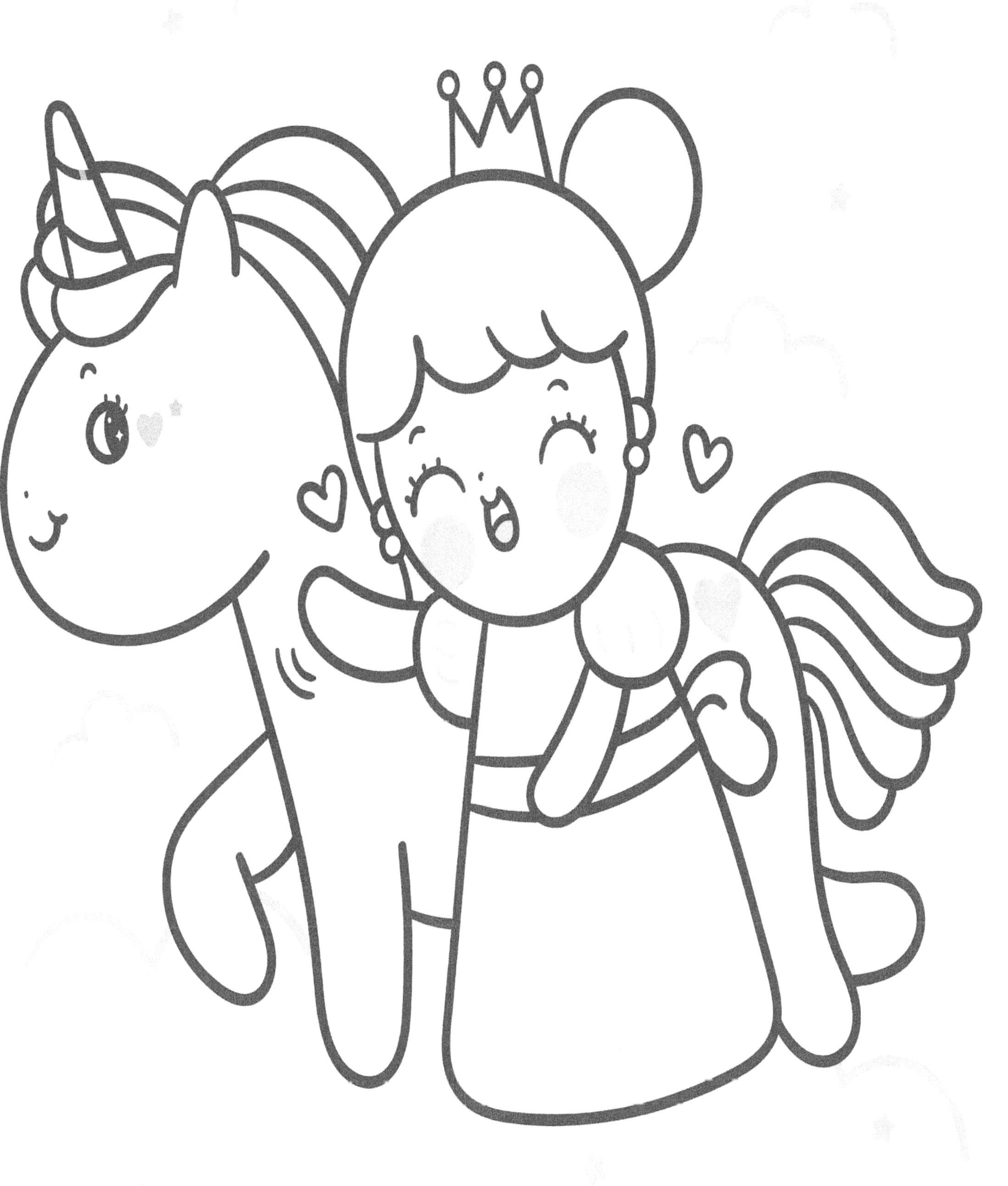

PRETTY UNICORN SET

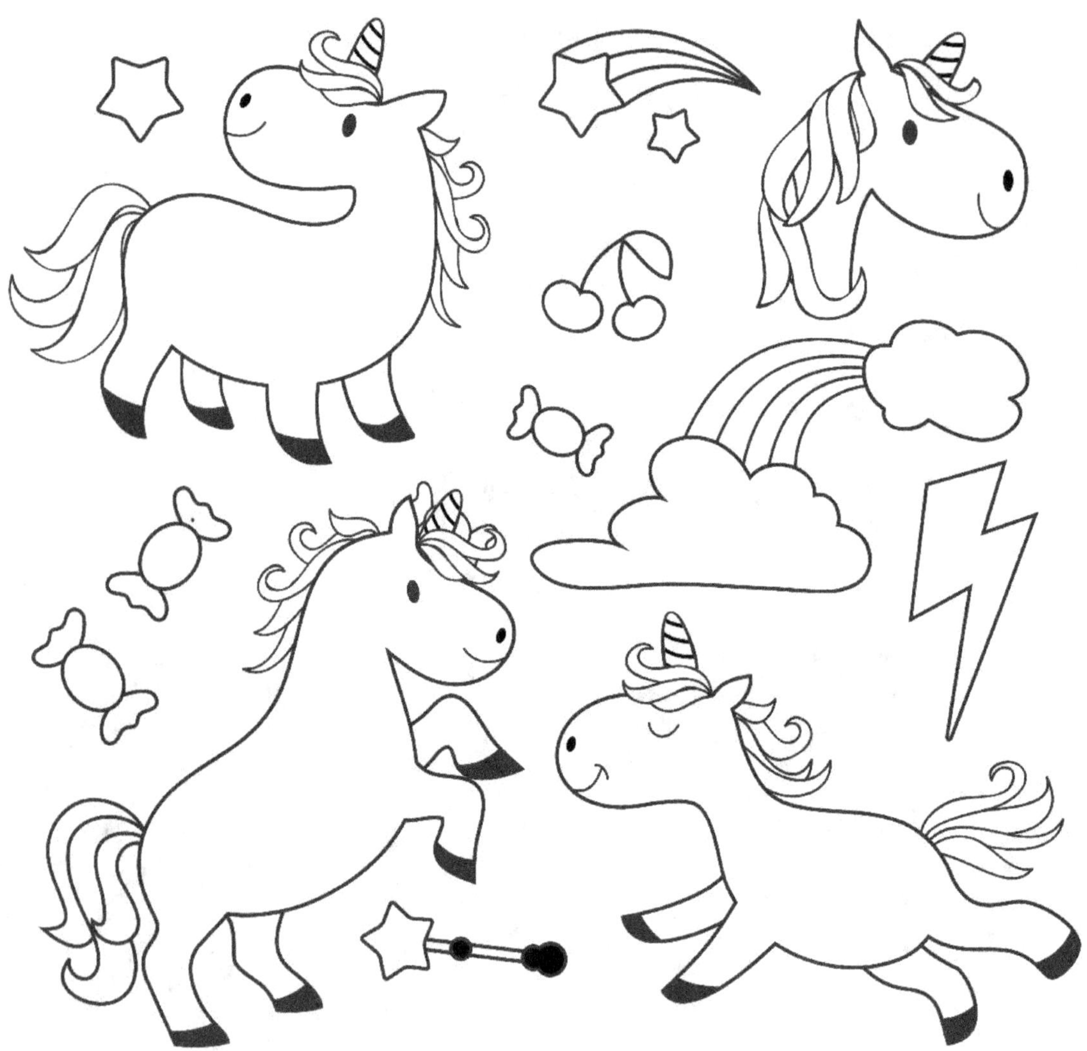

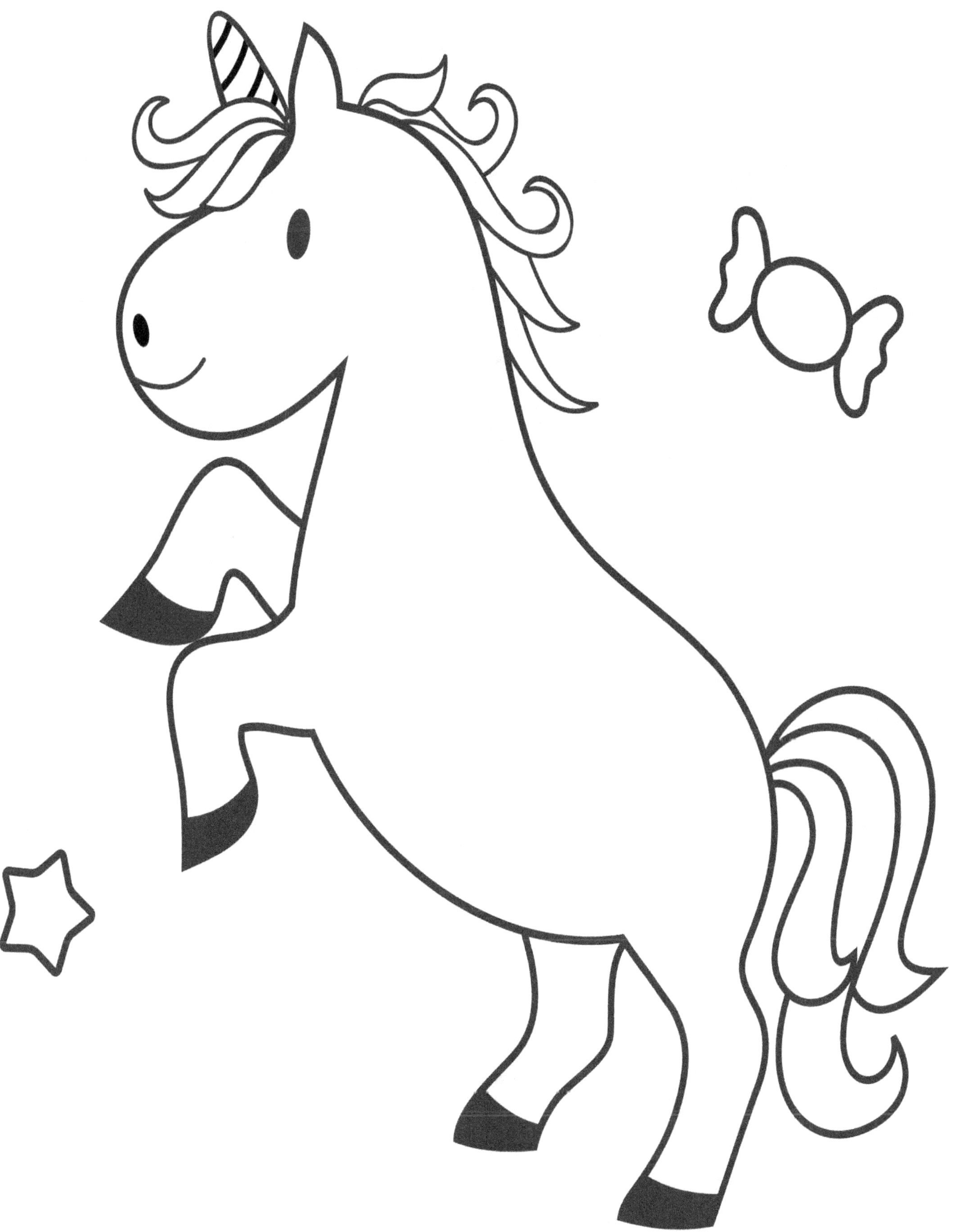

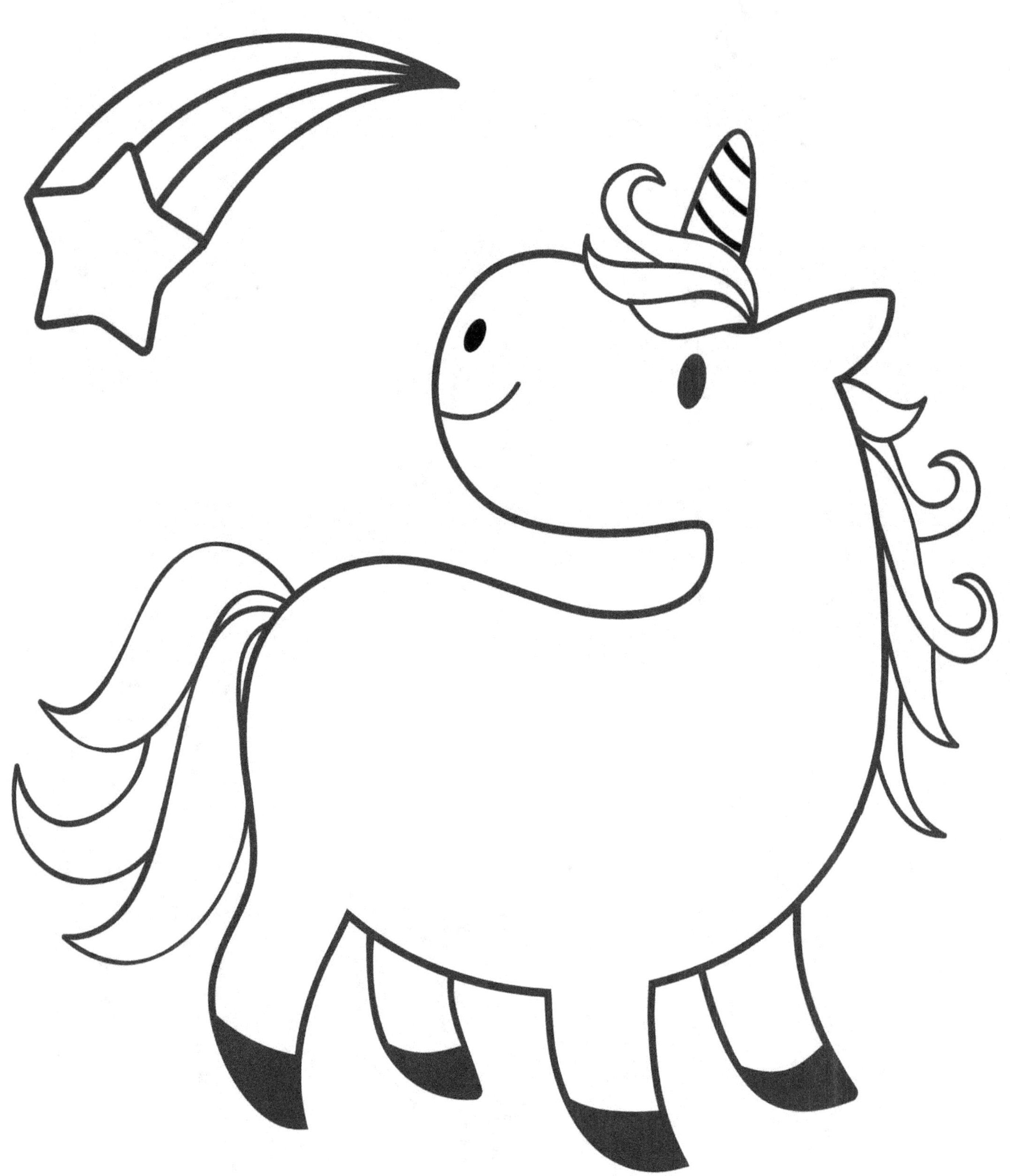

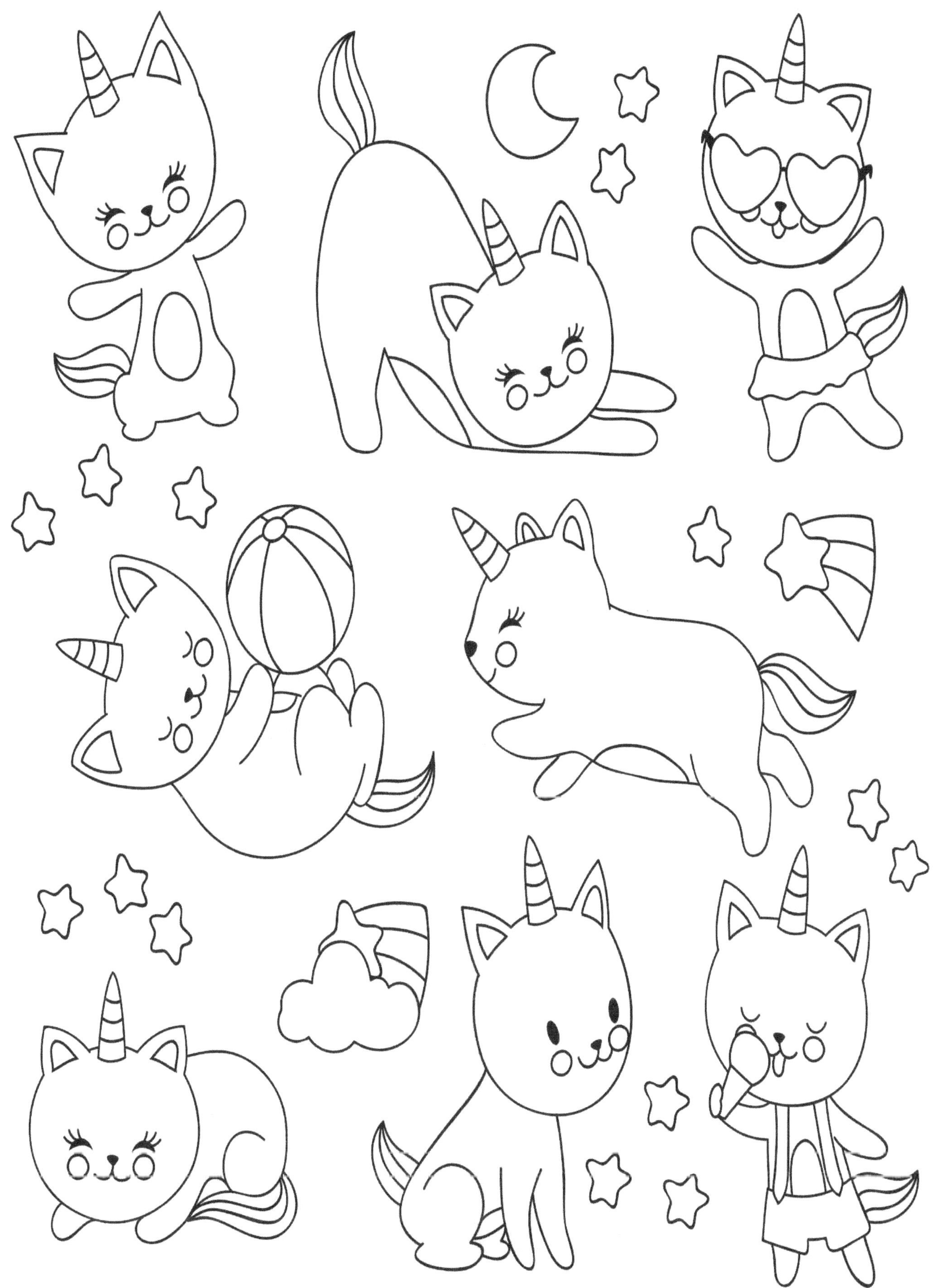

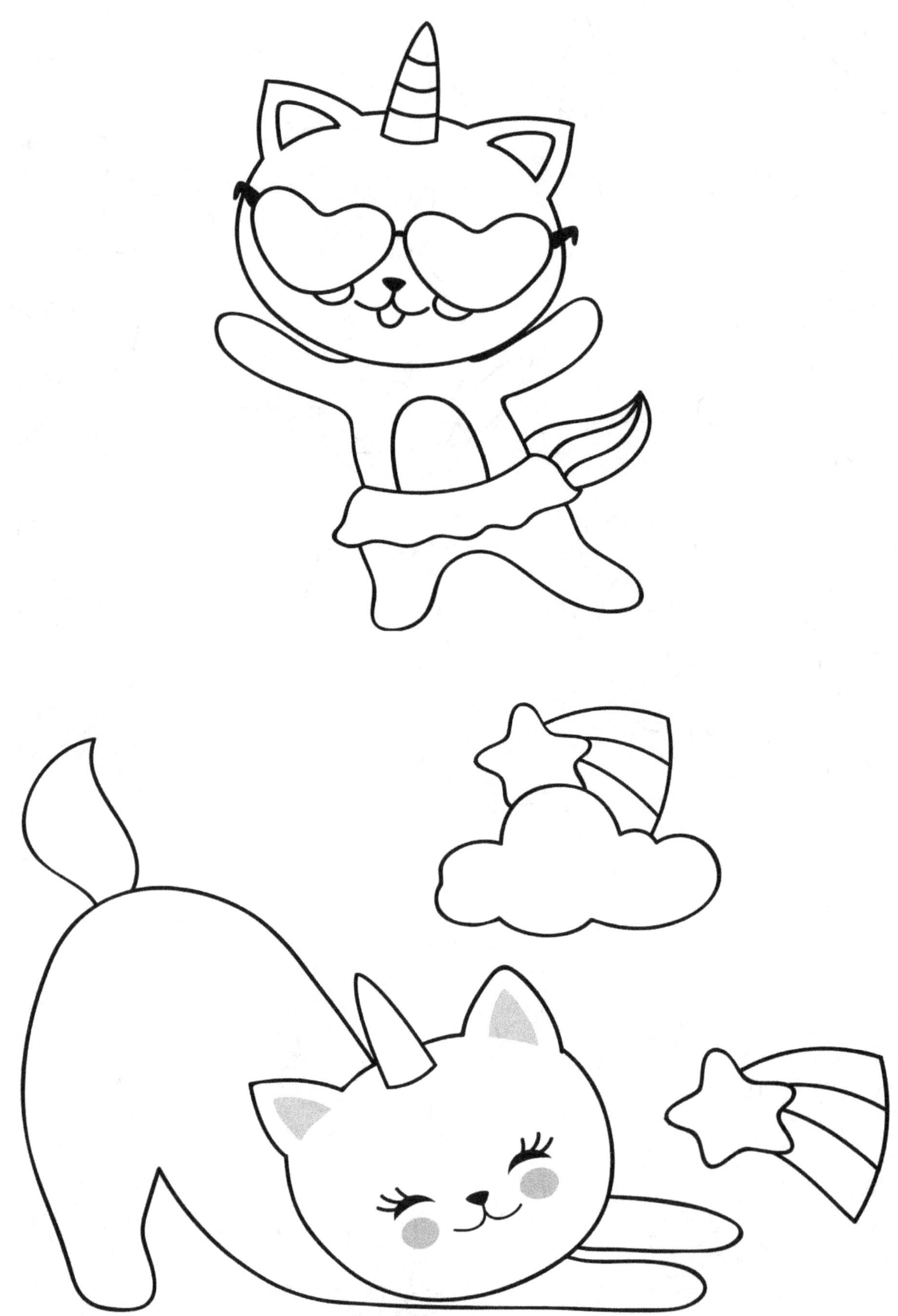

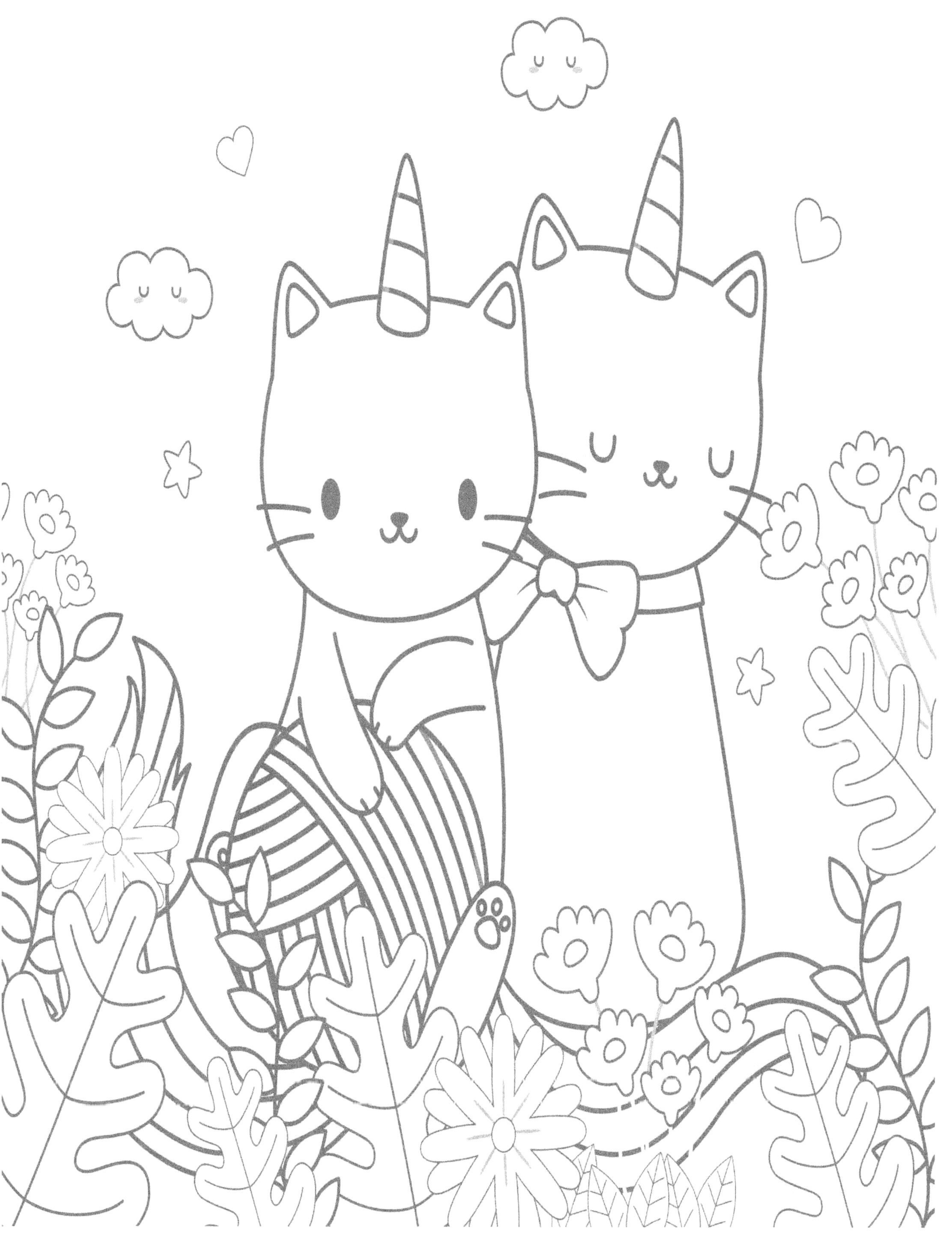

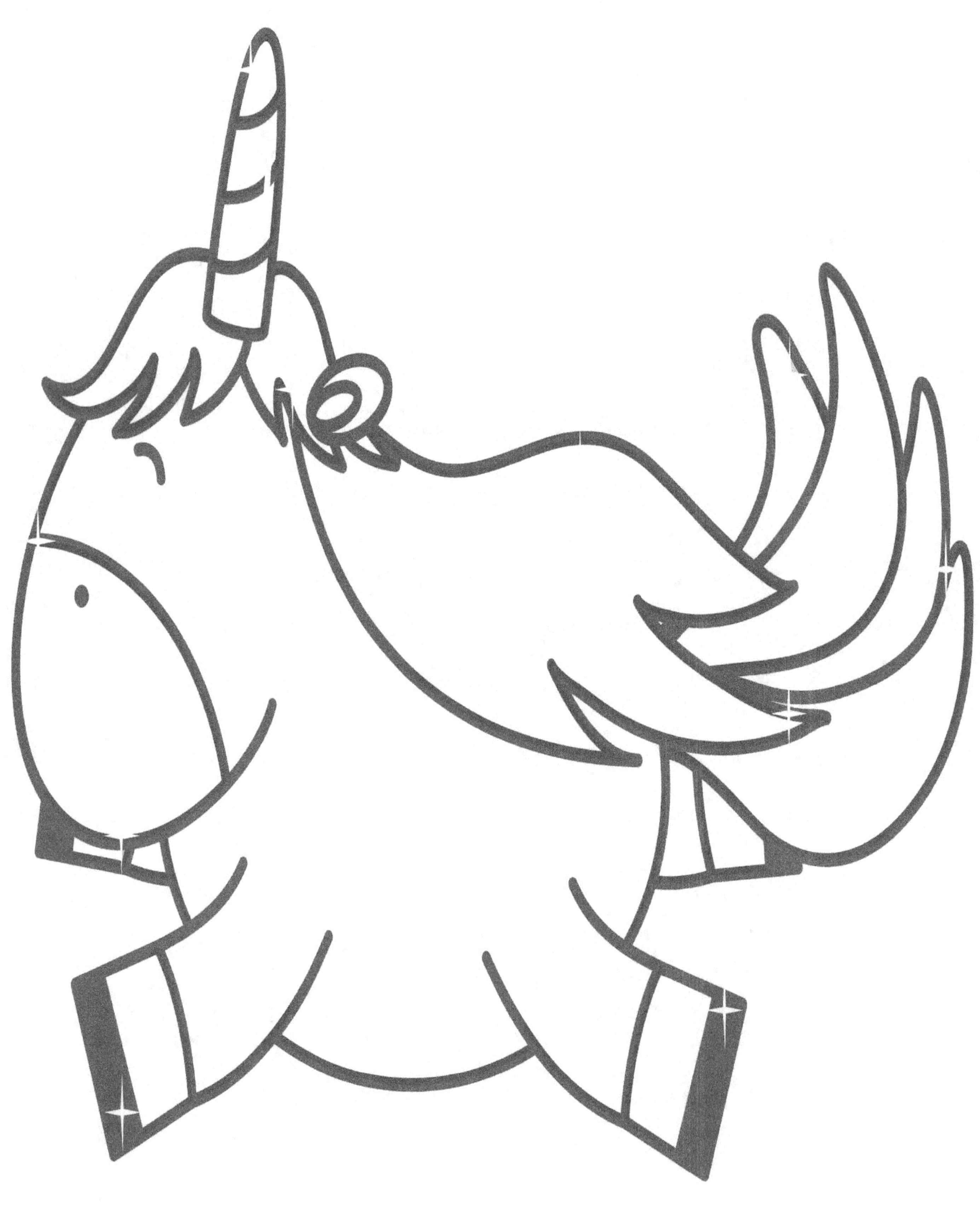

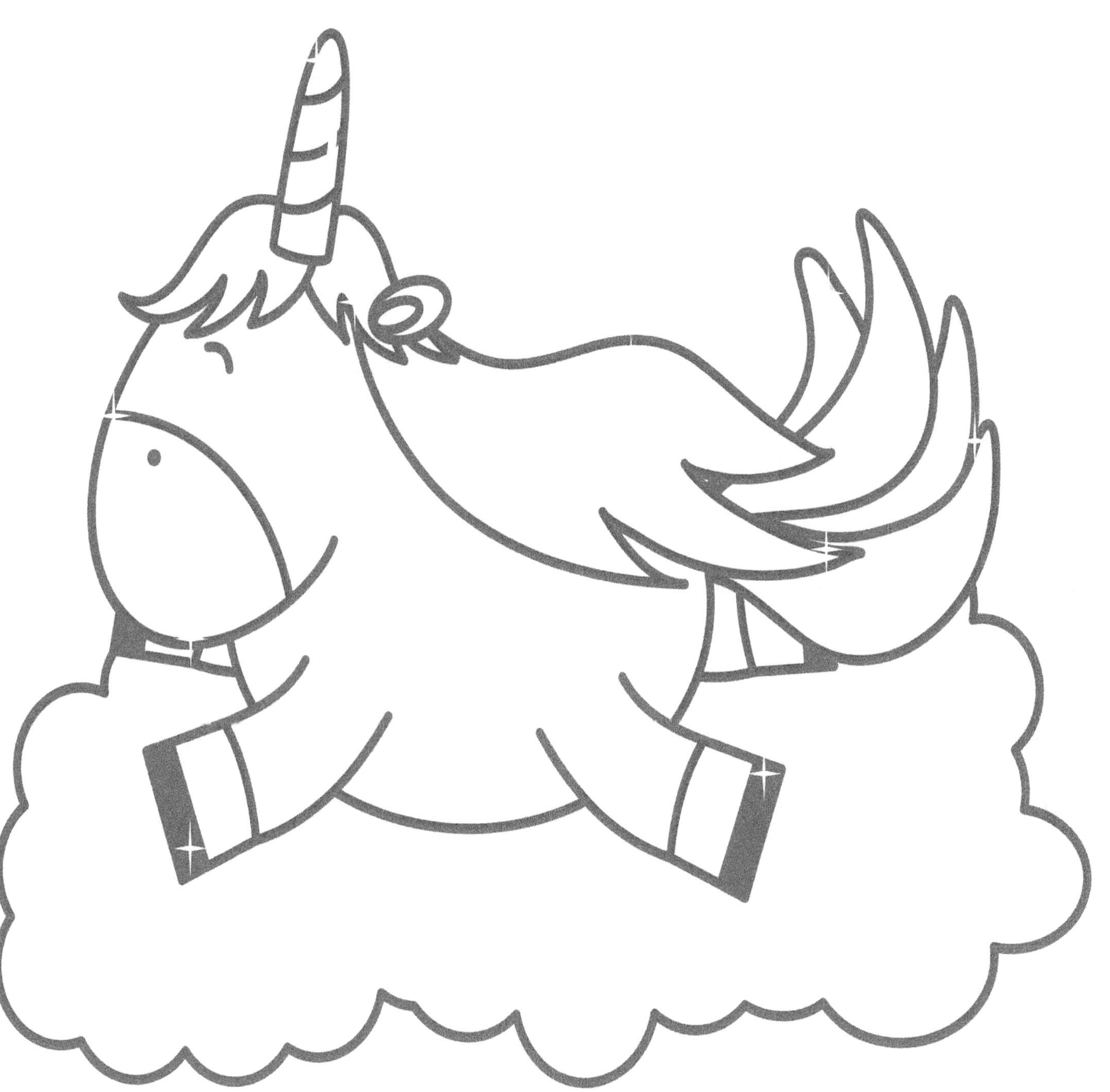

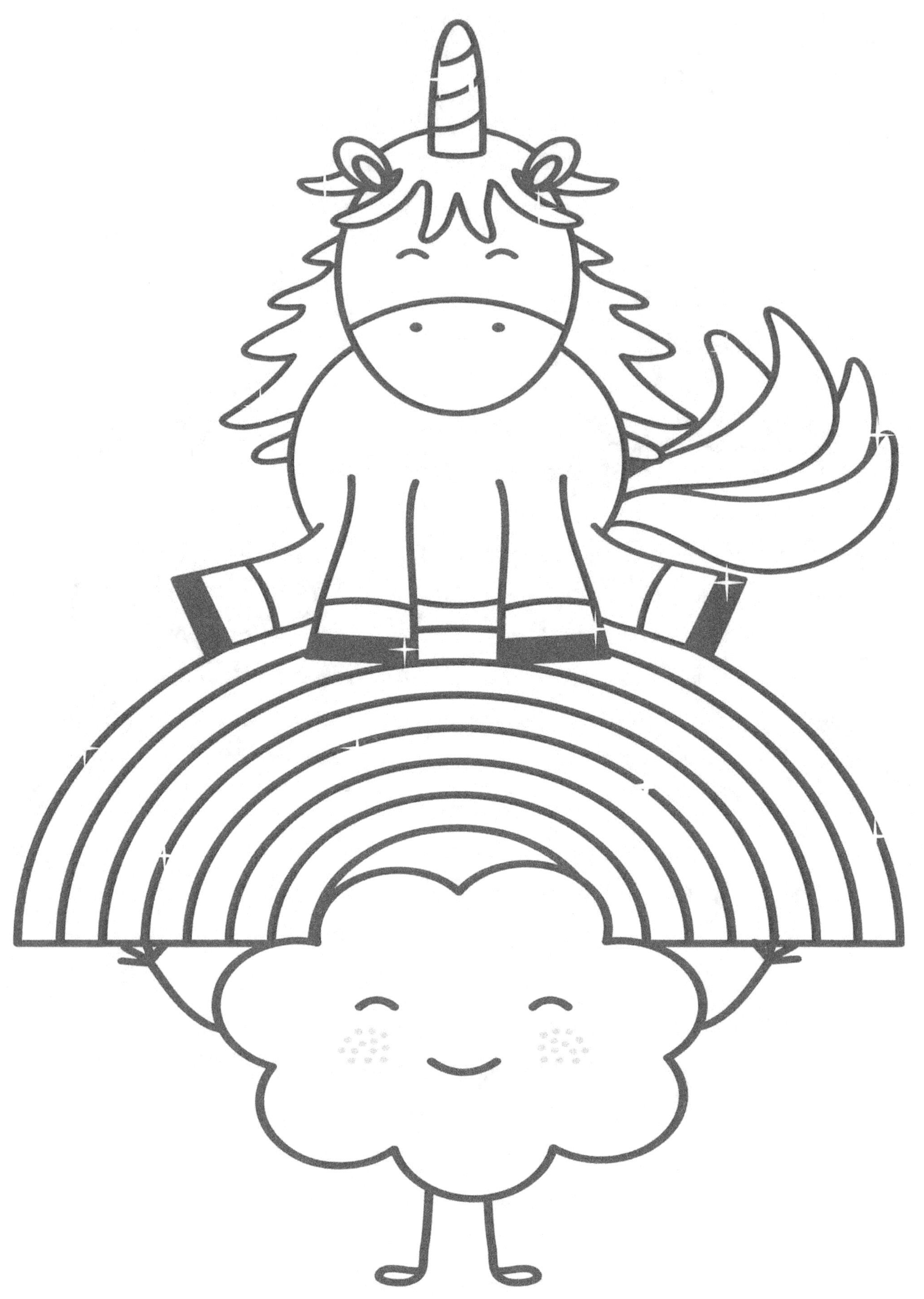

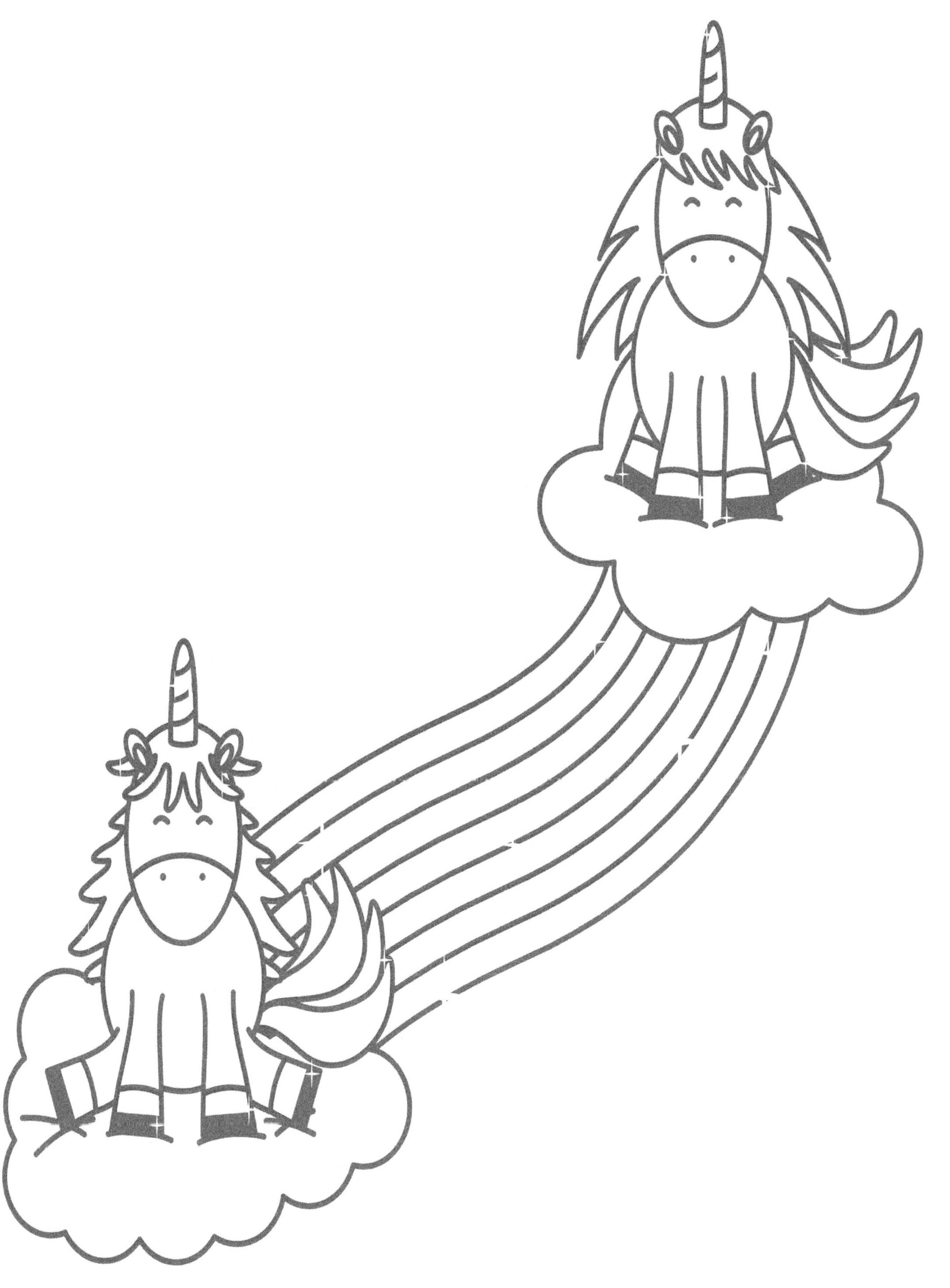

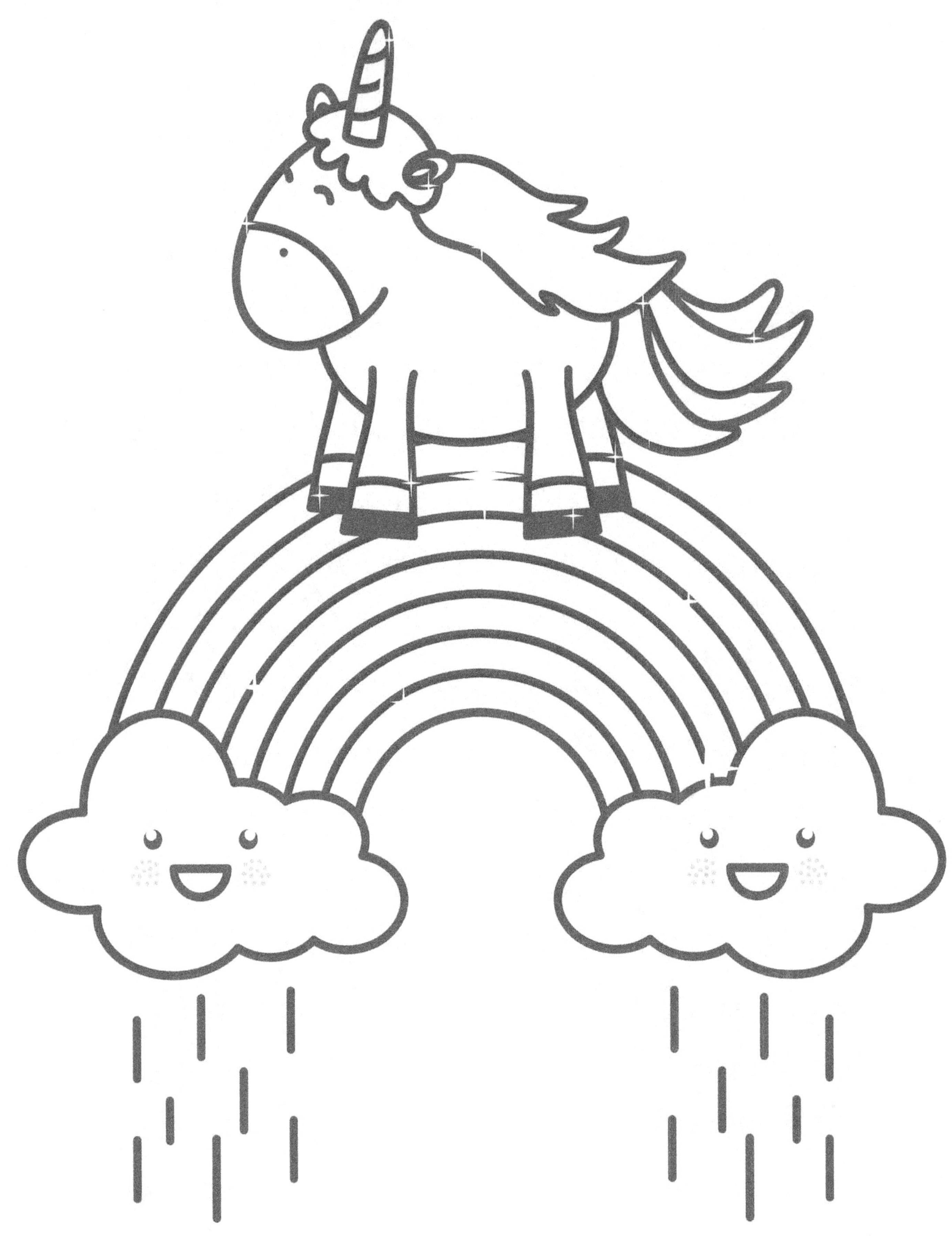

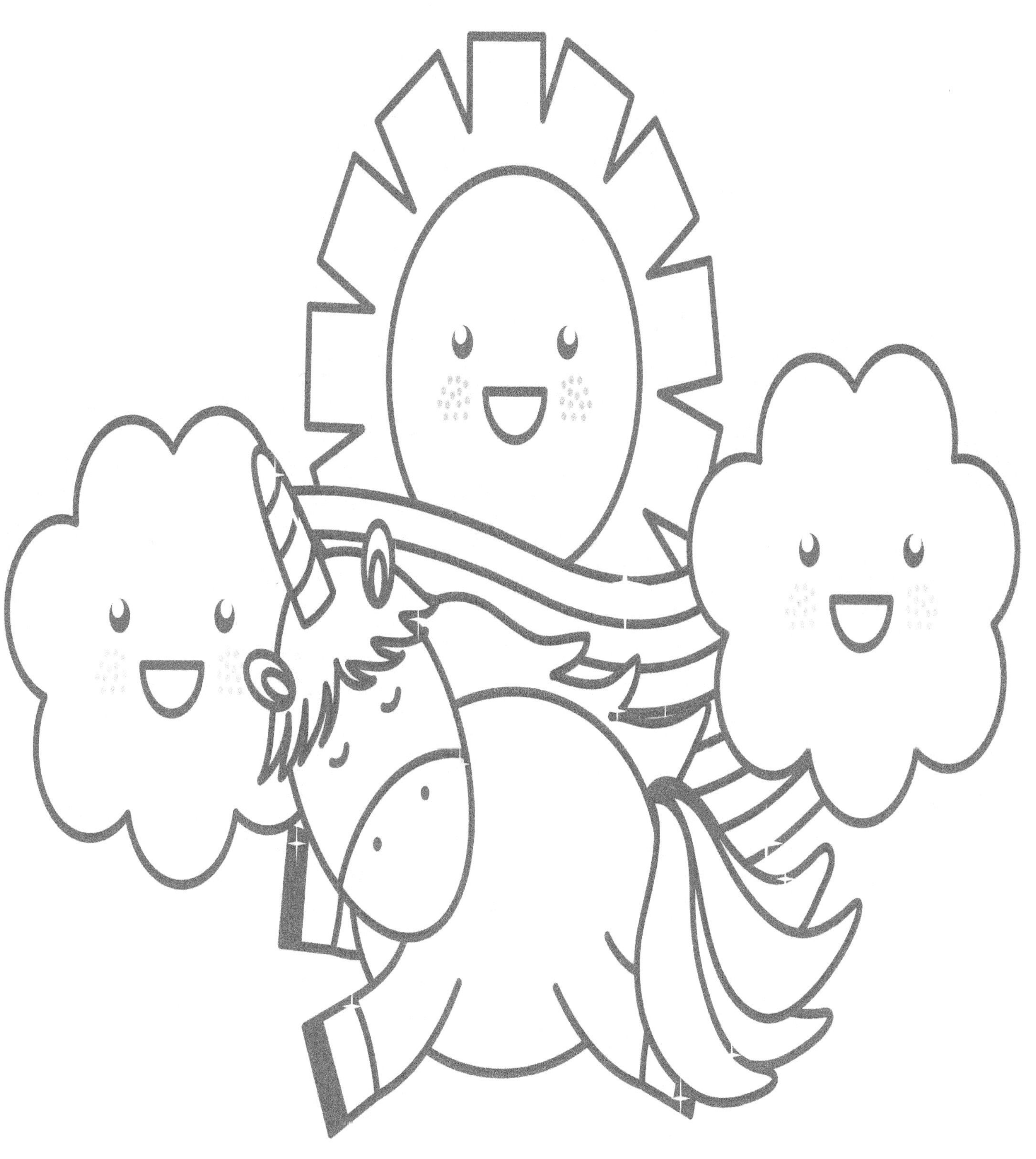

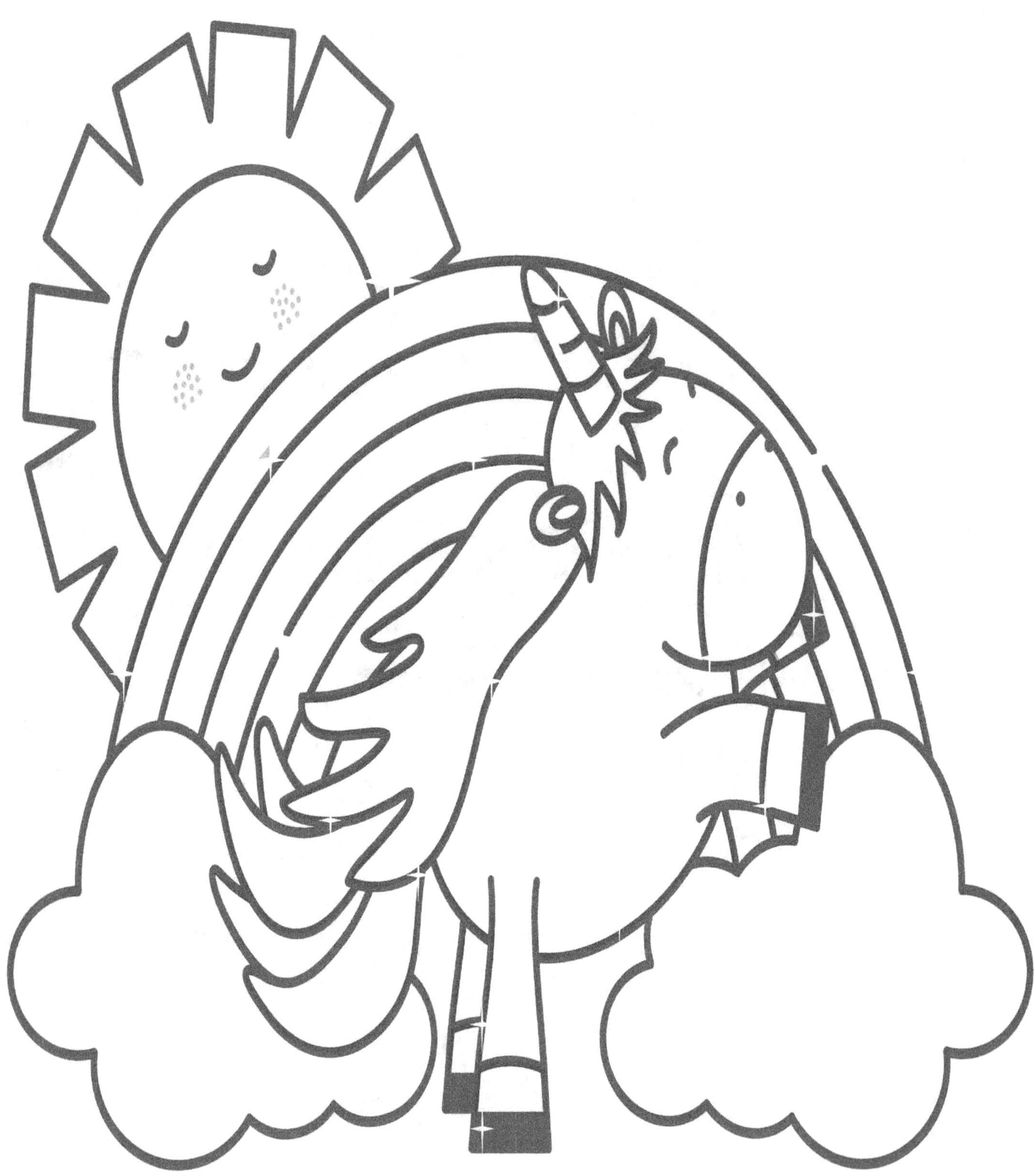

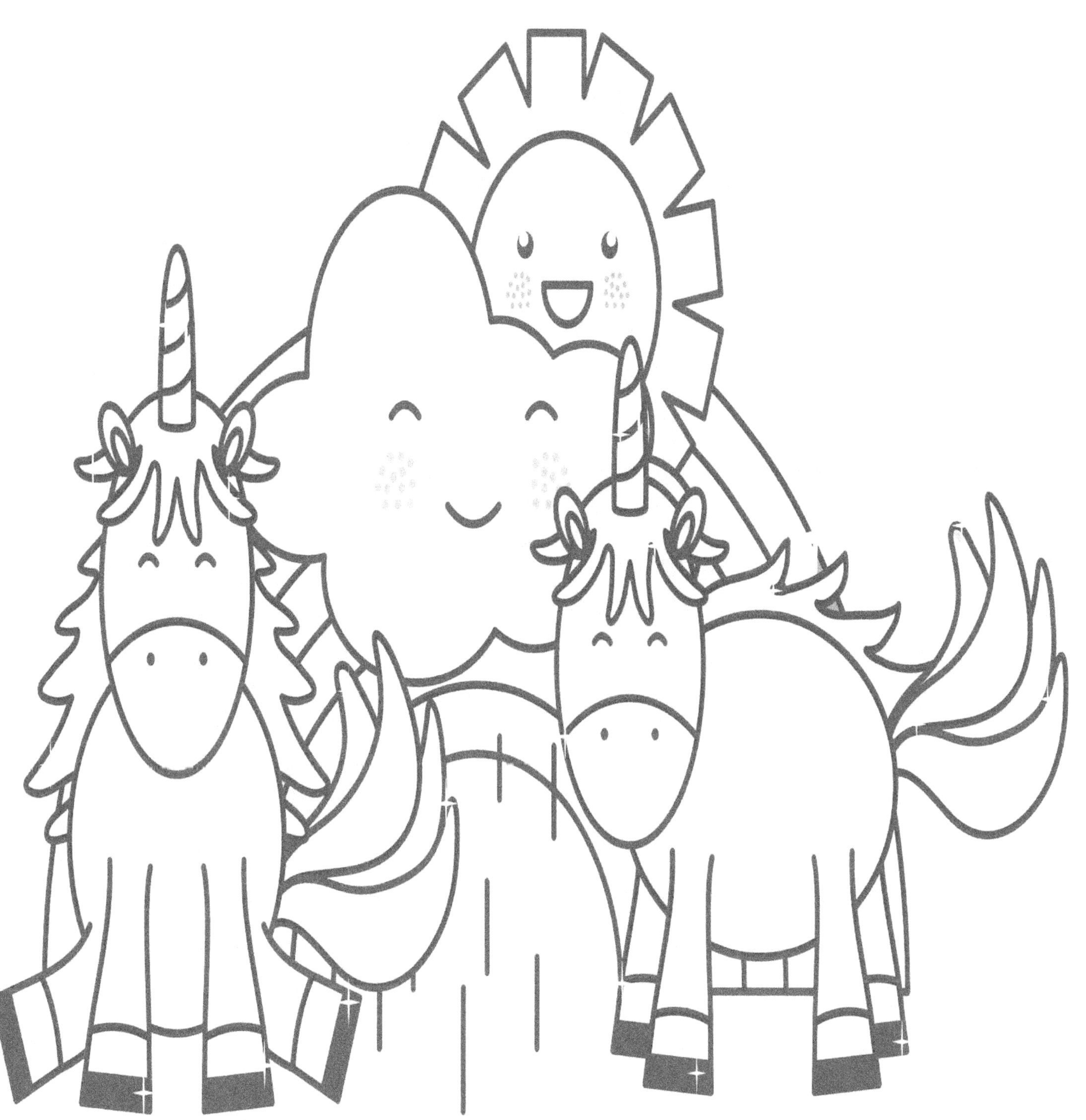

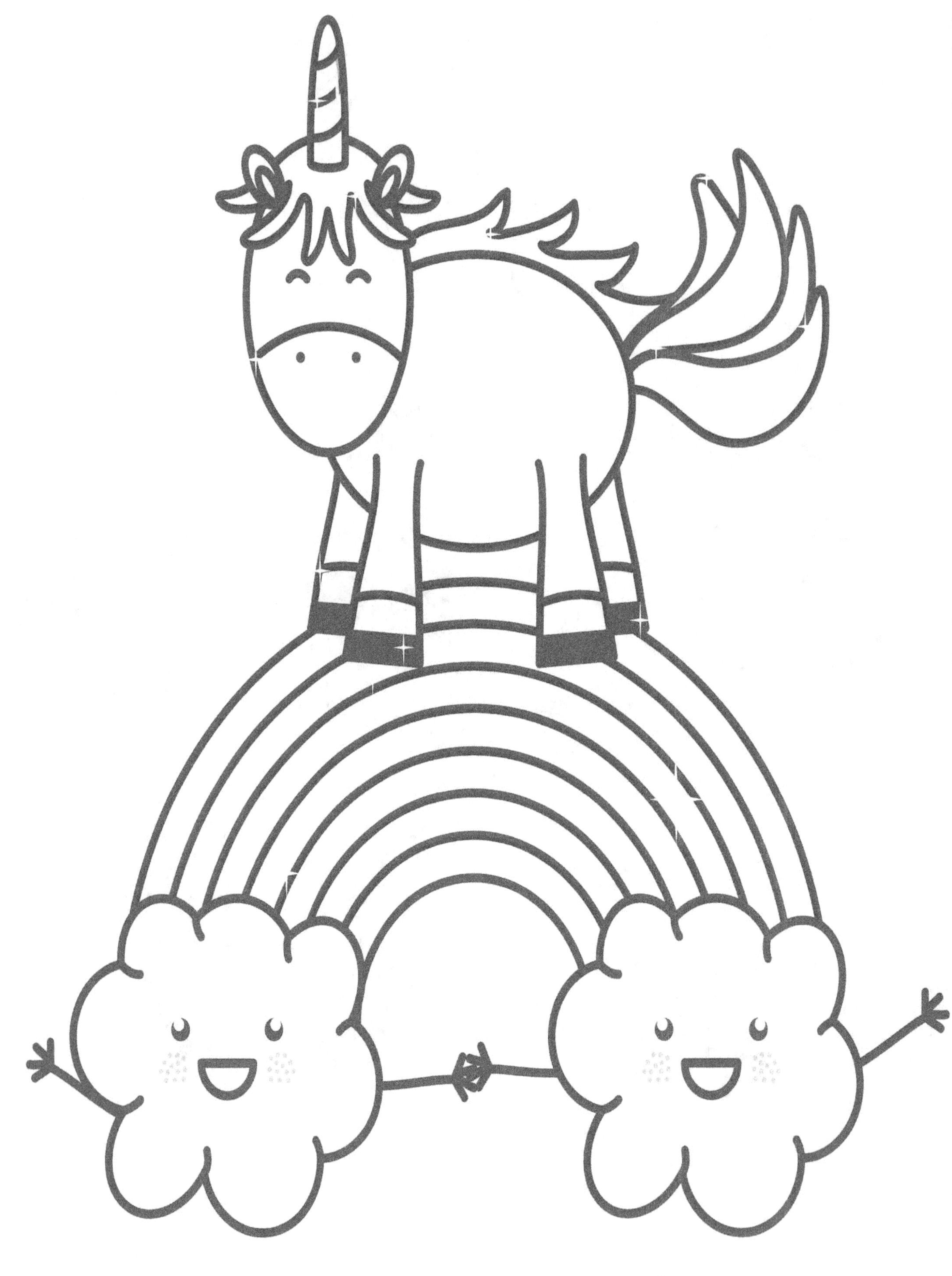

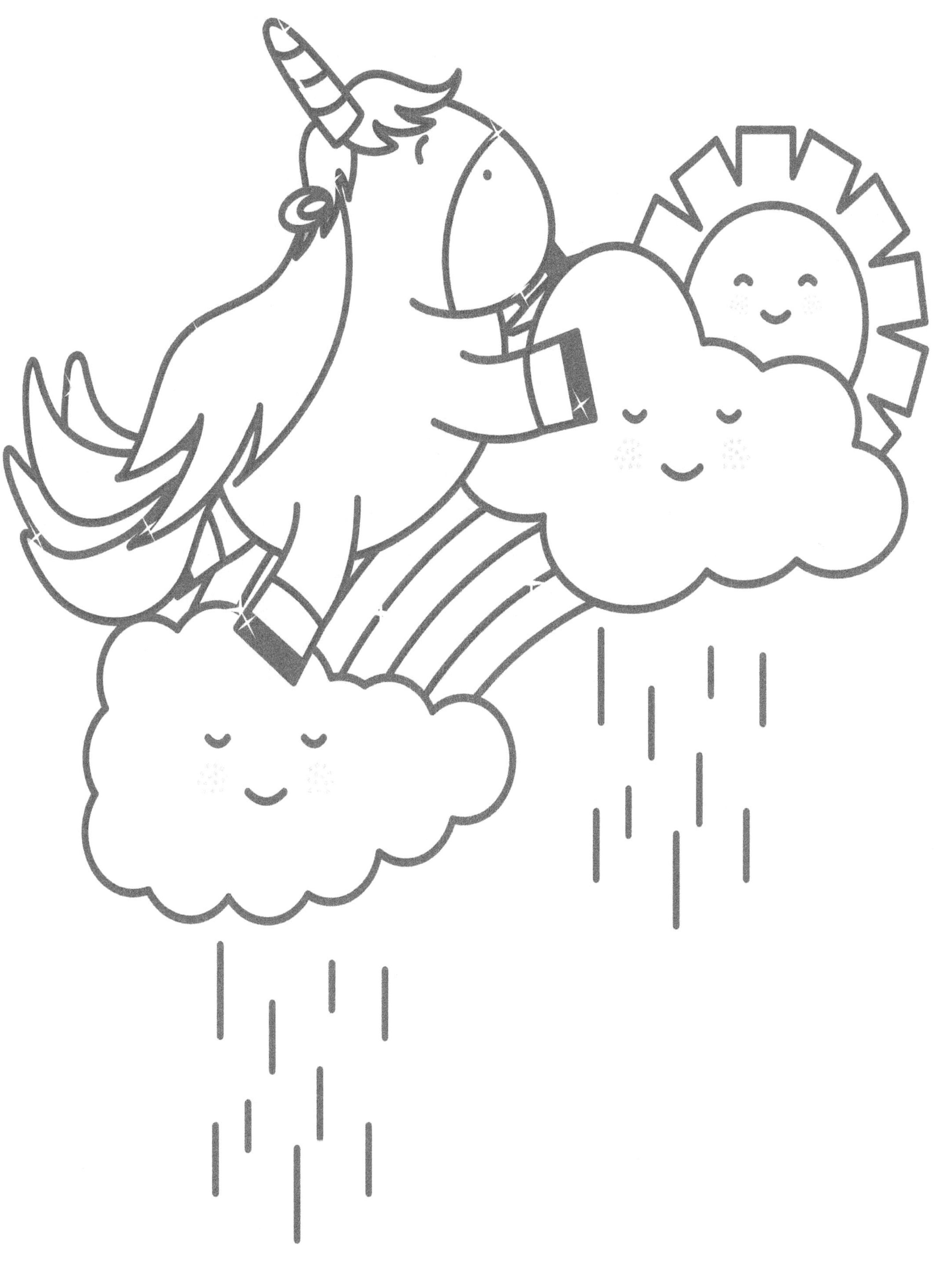

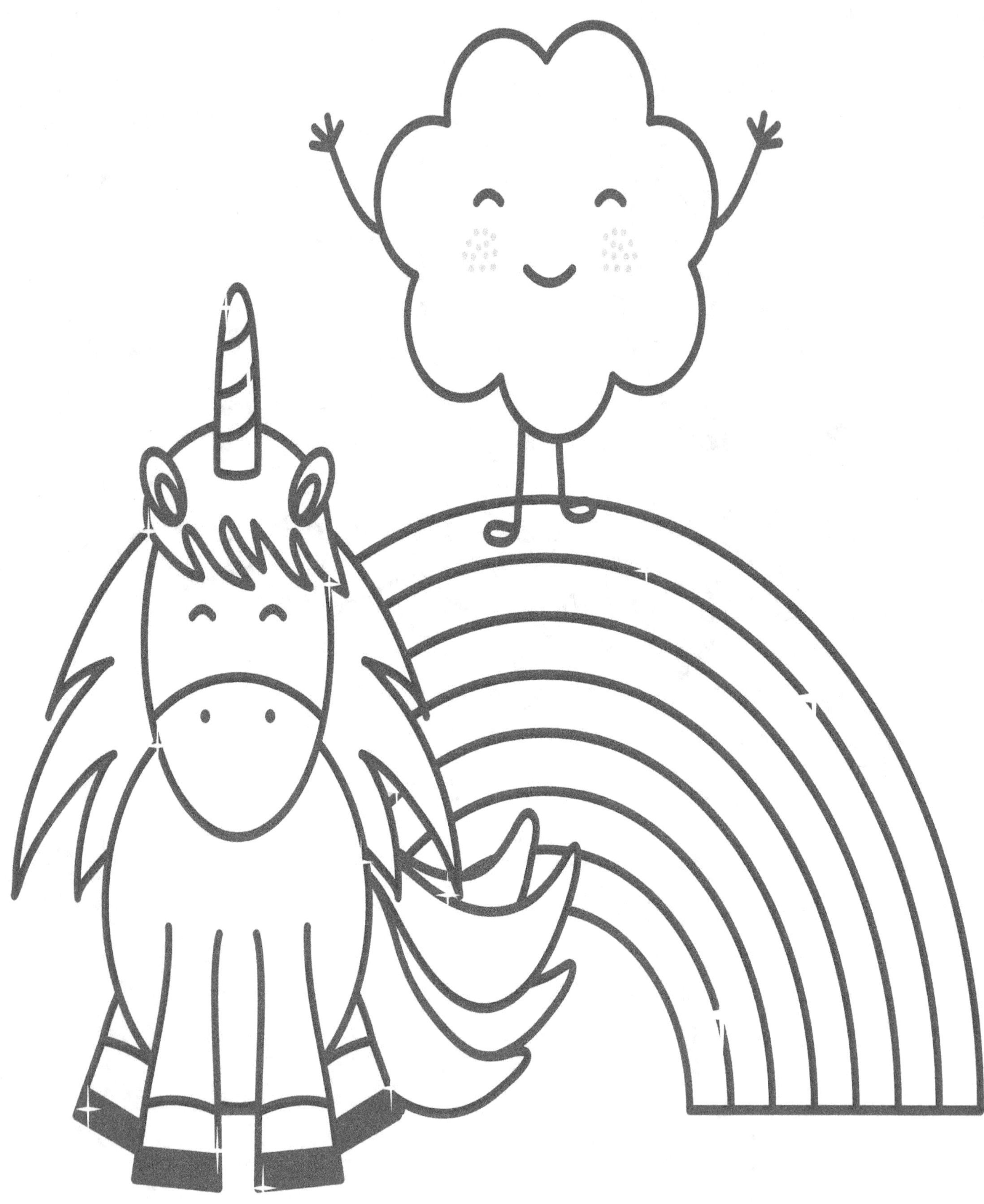

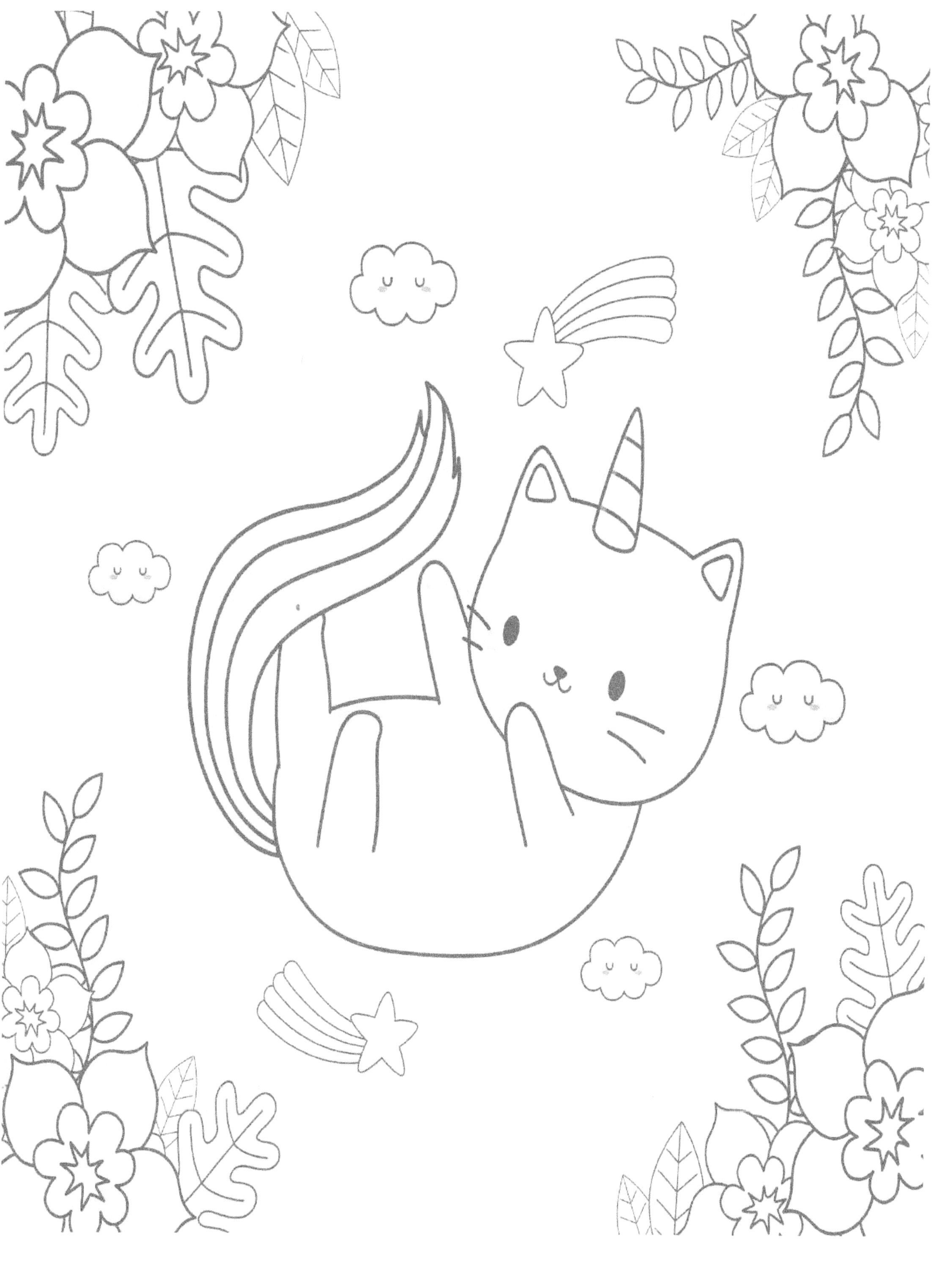

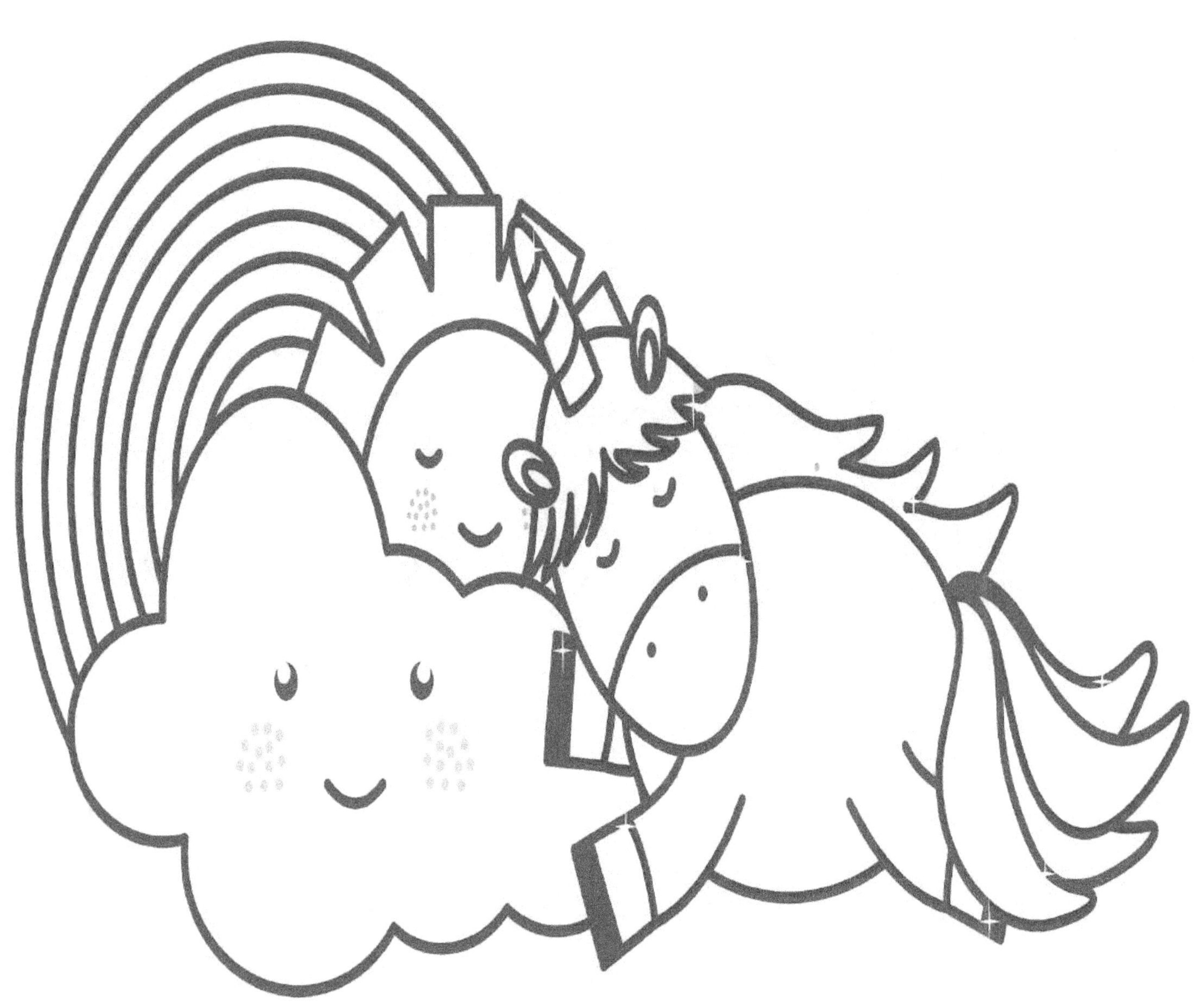

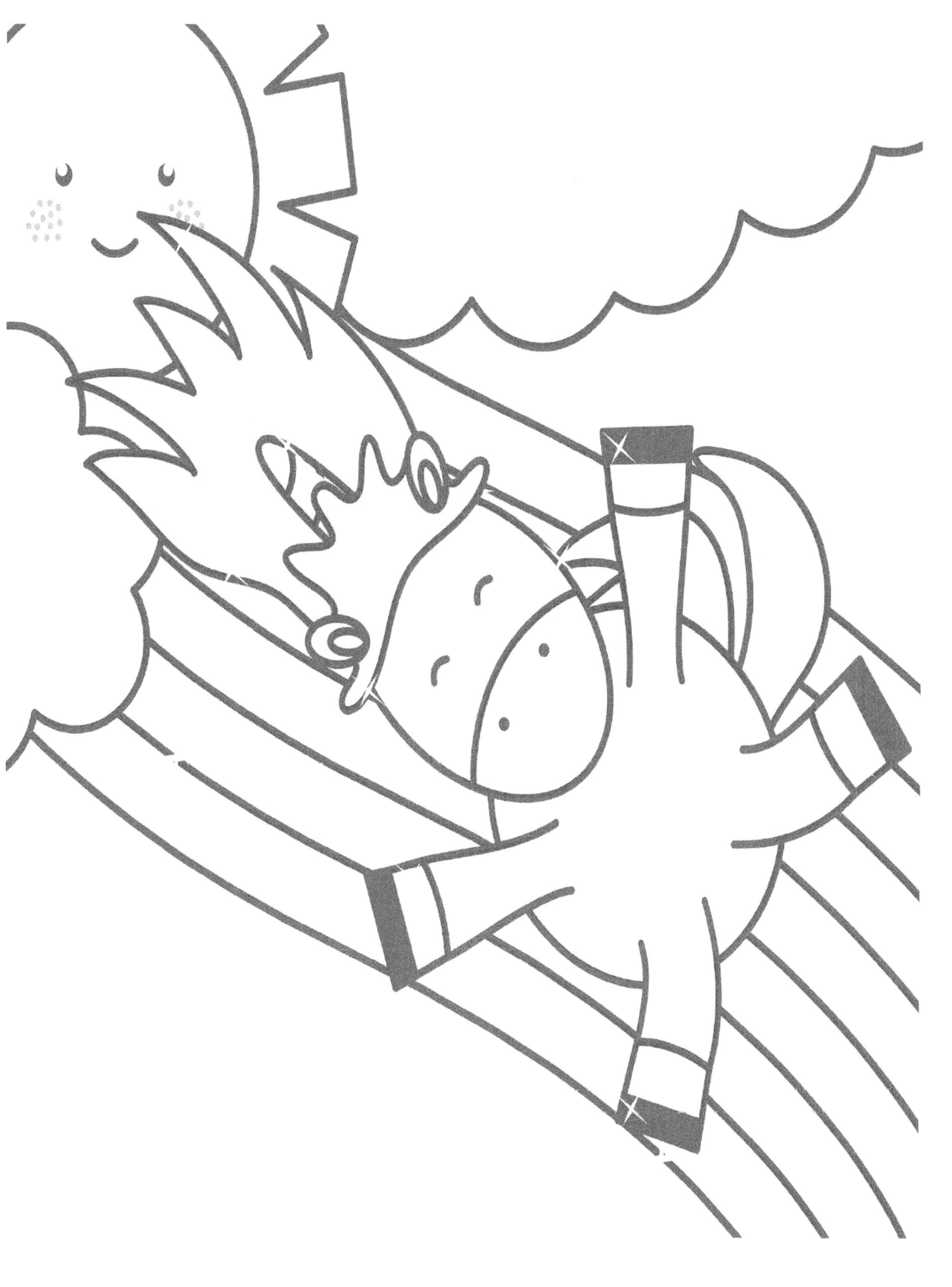

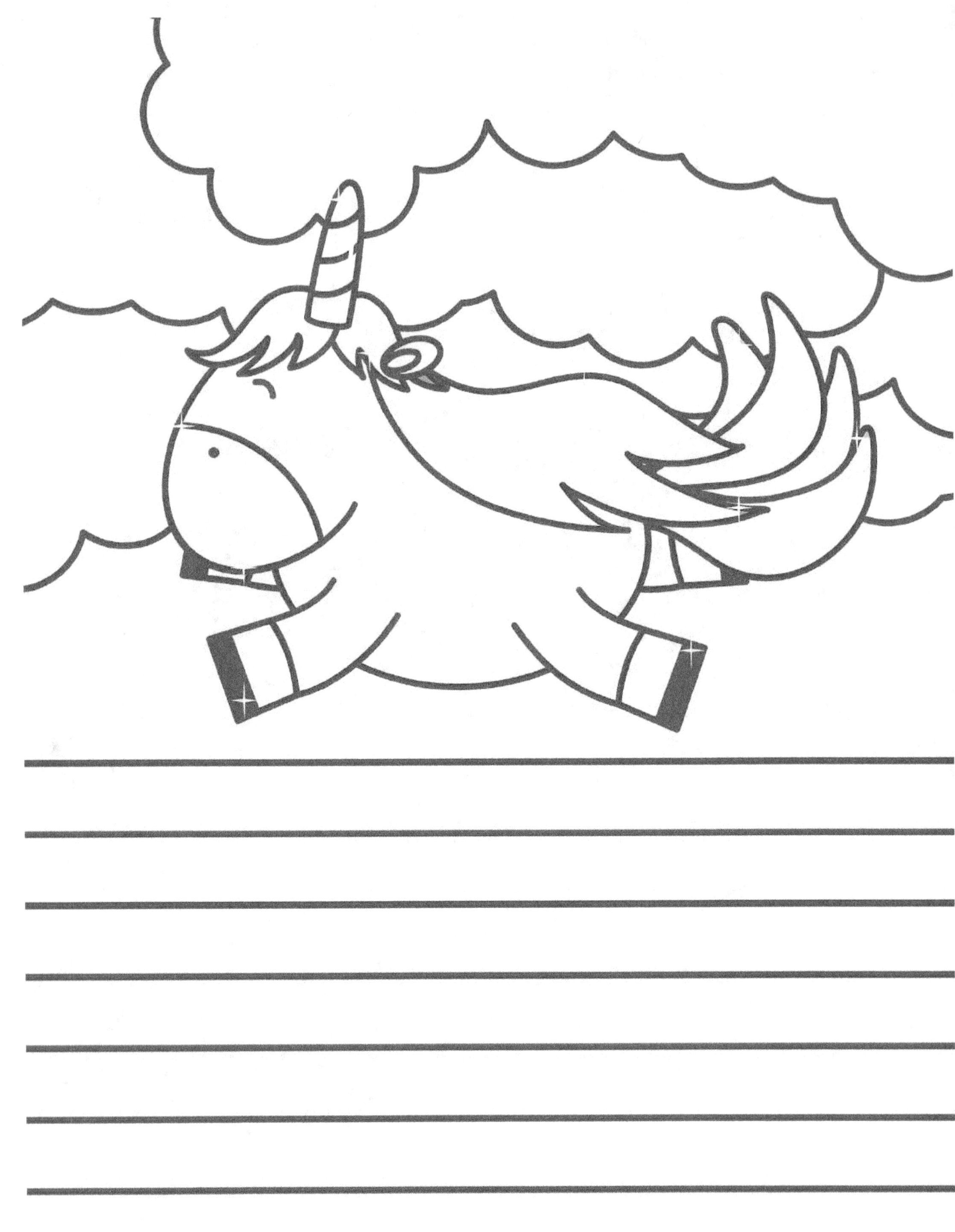

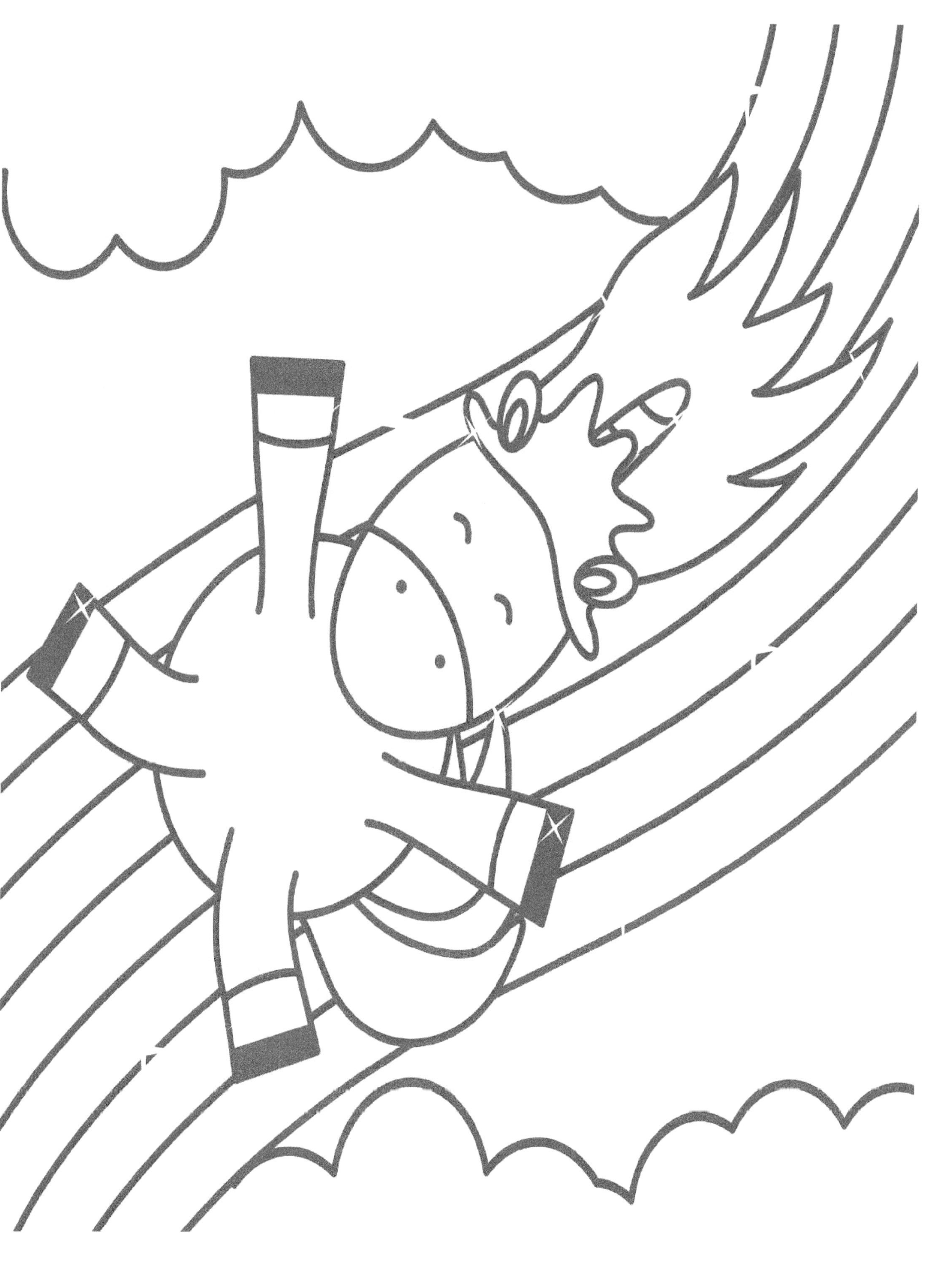

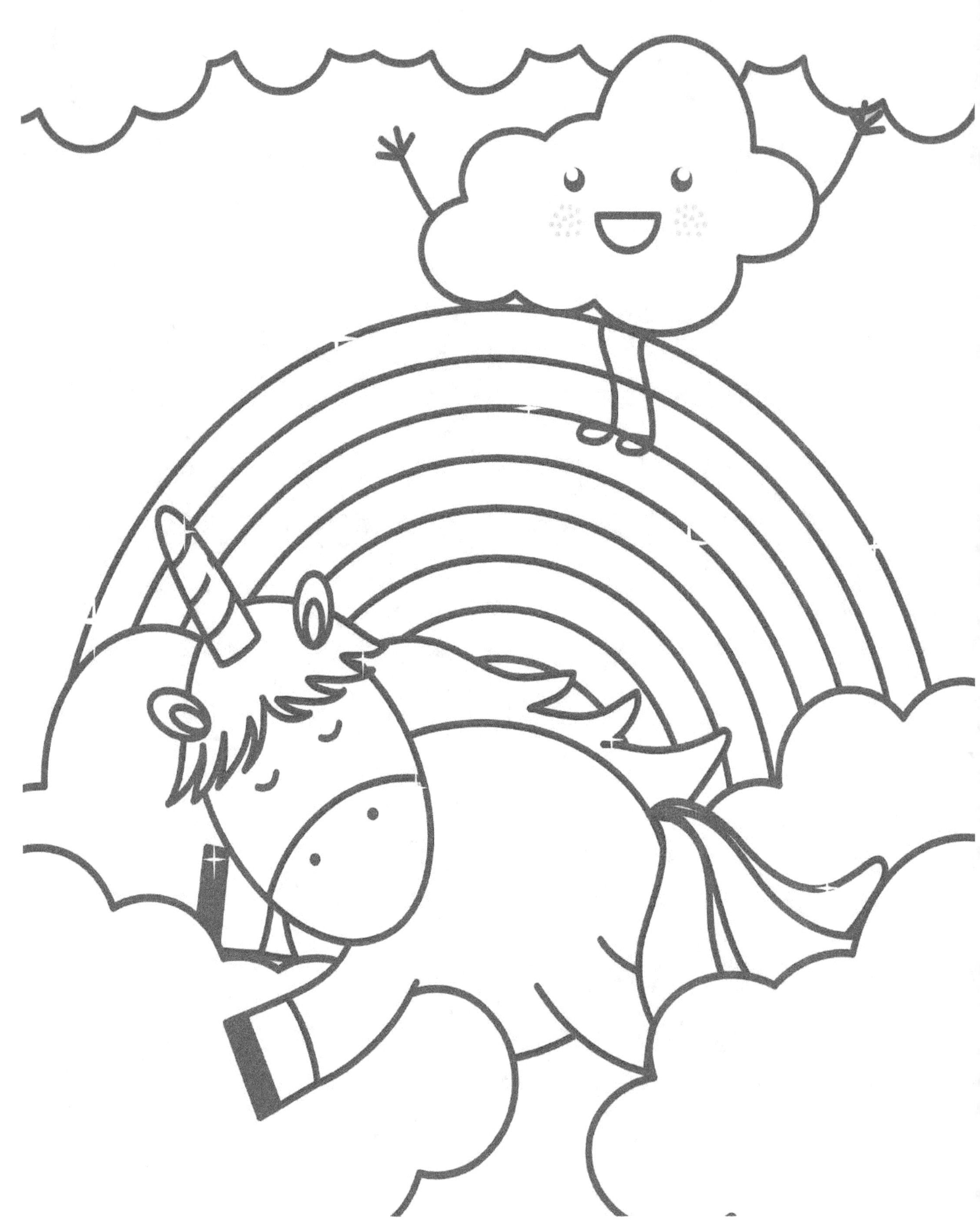

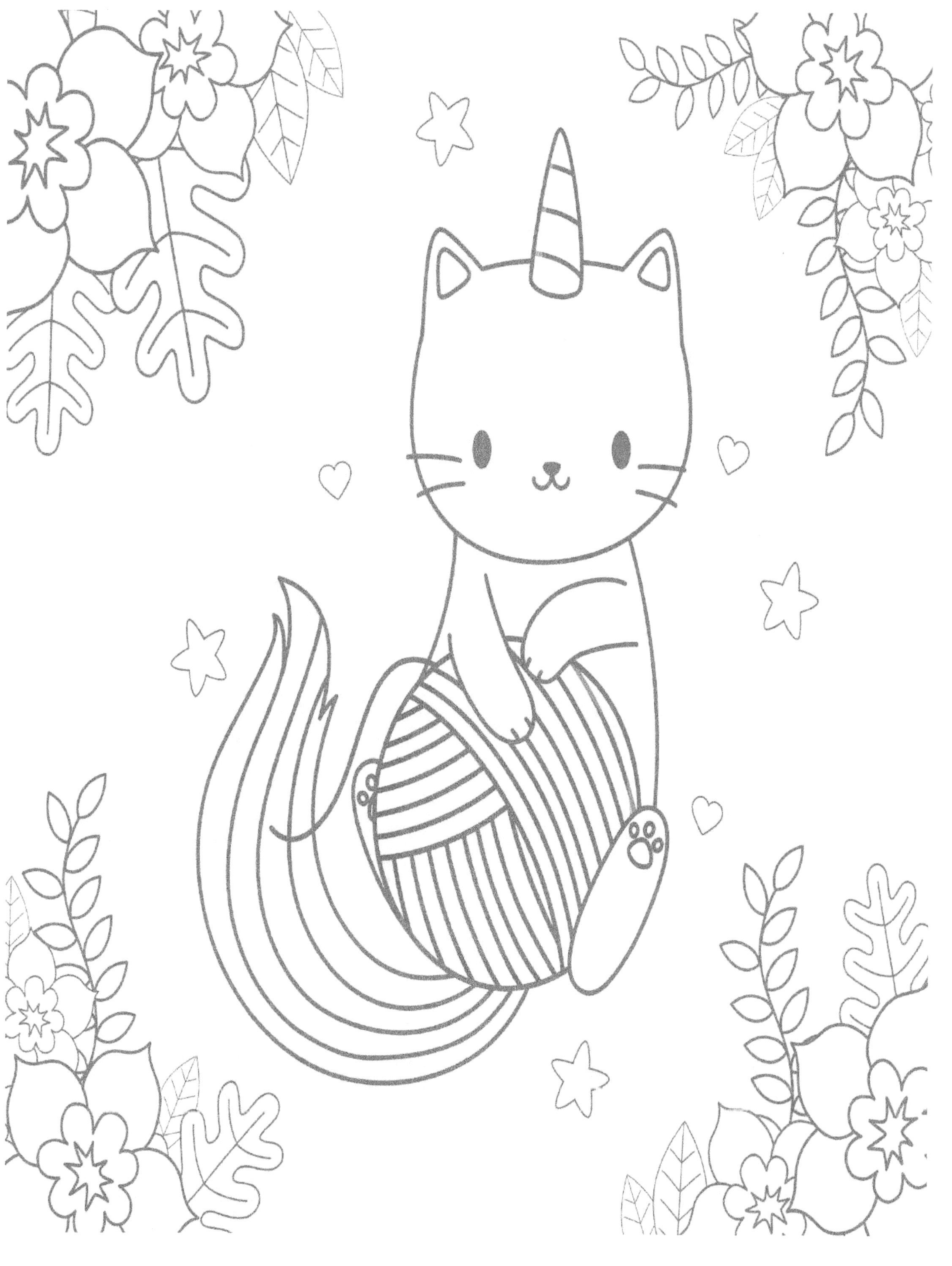

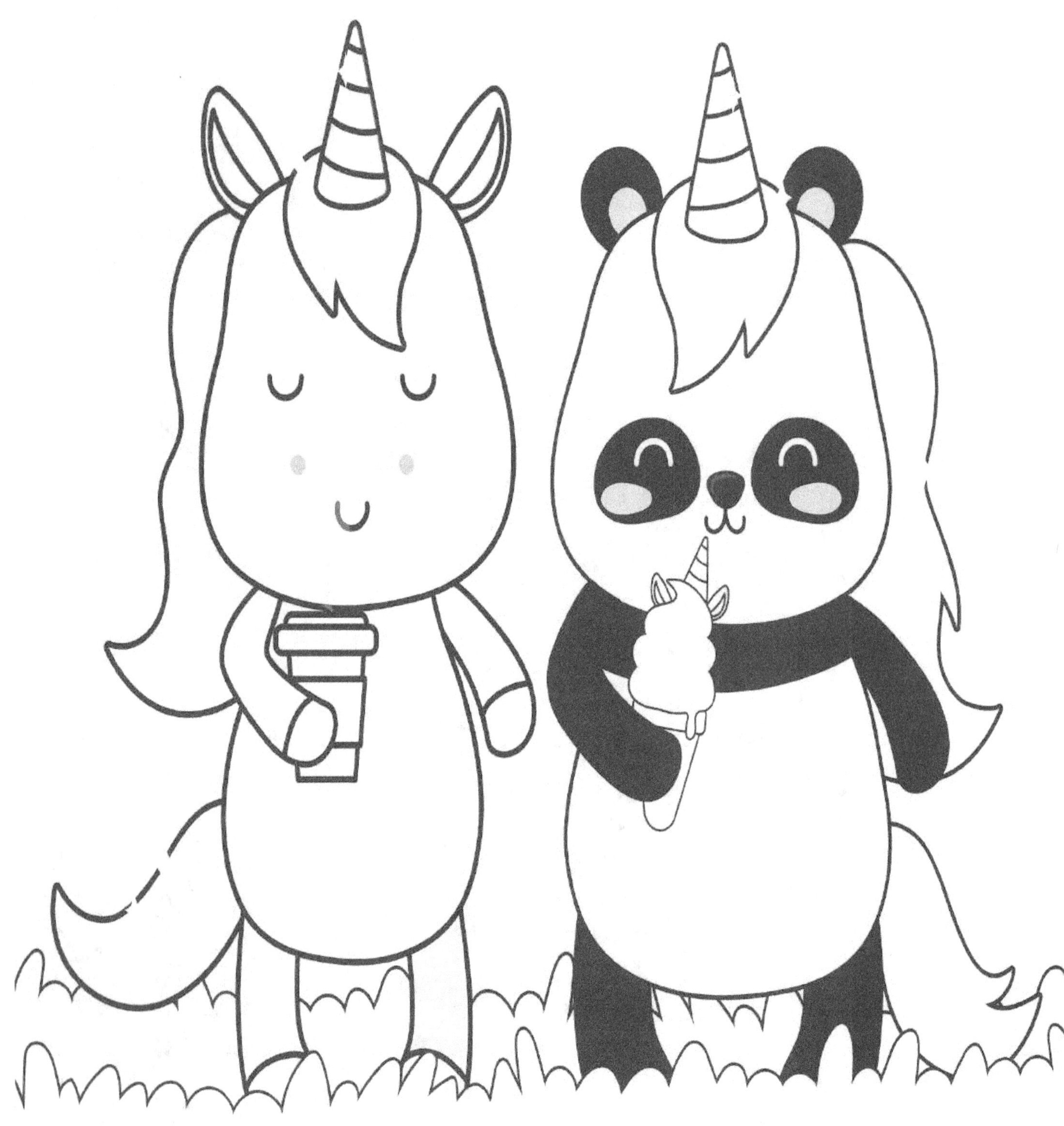

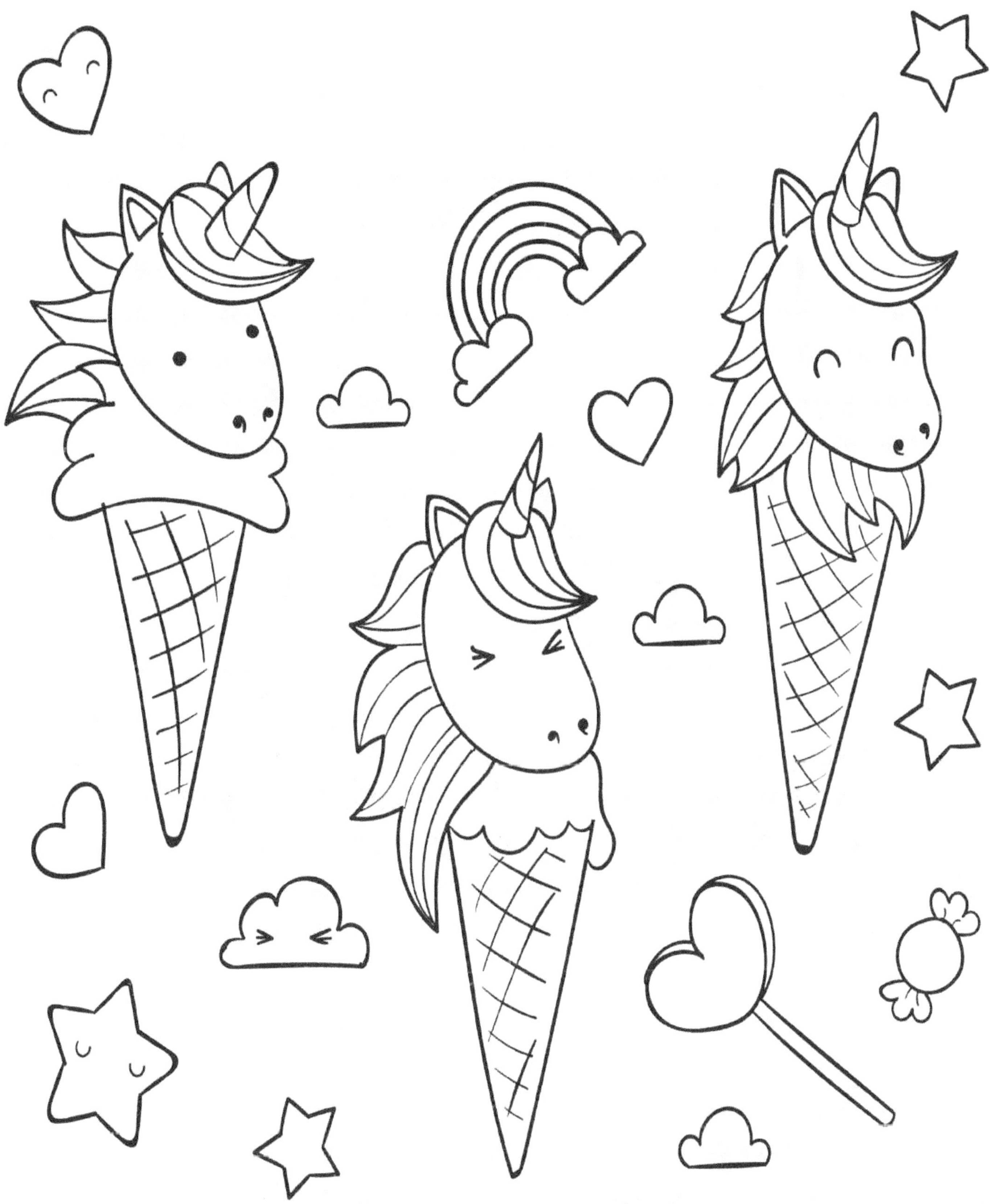

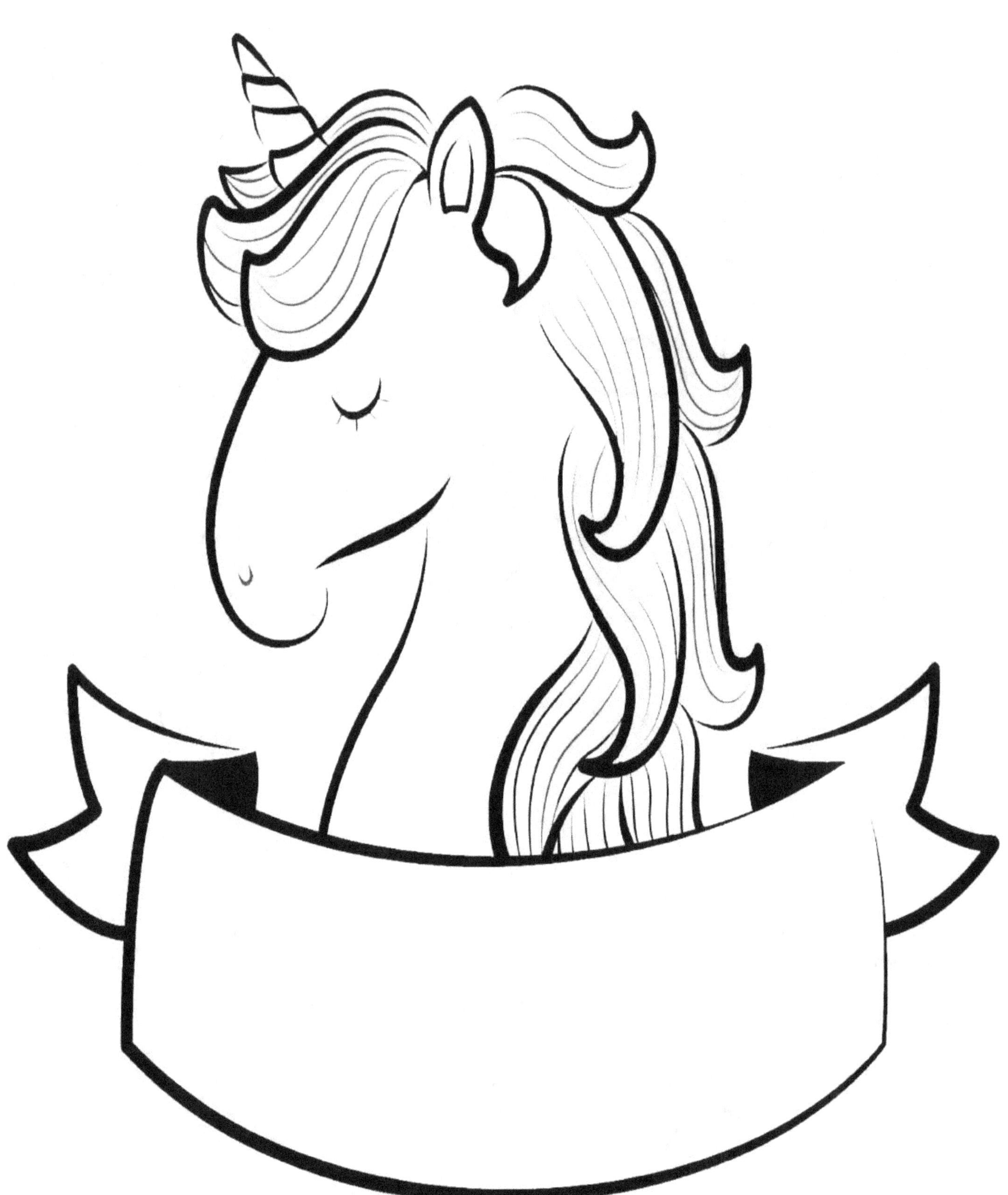

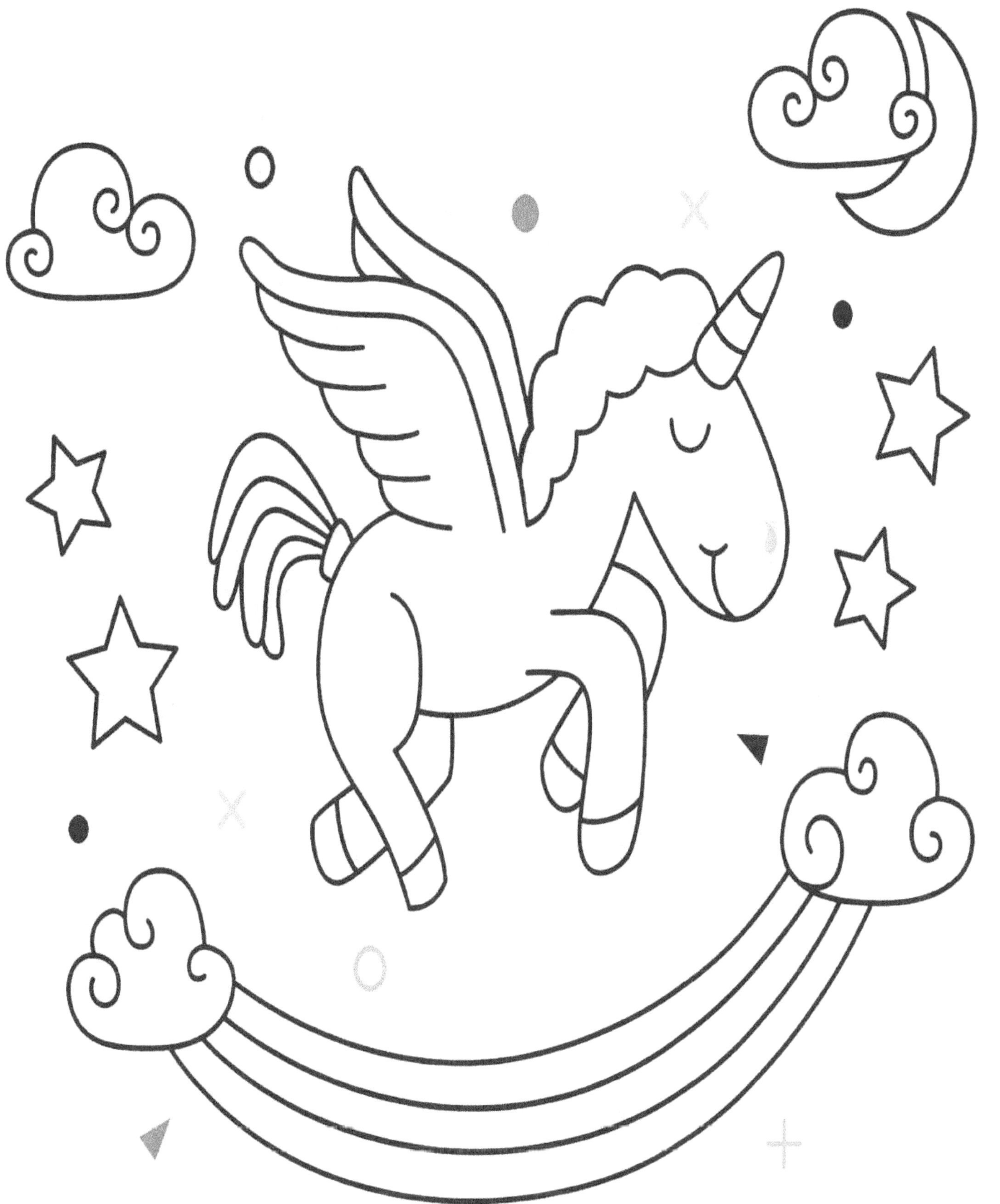

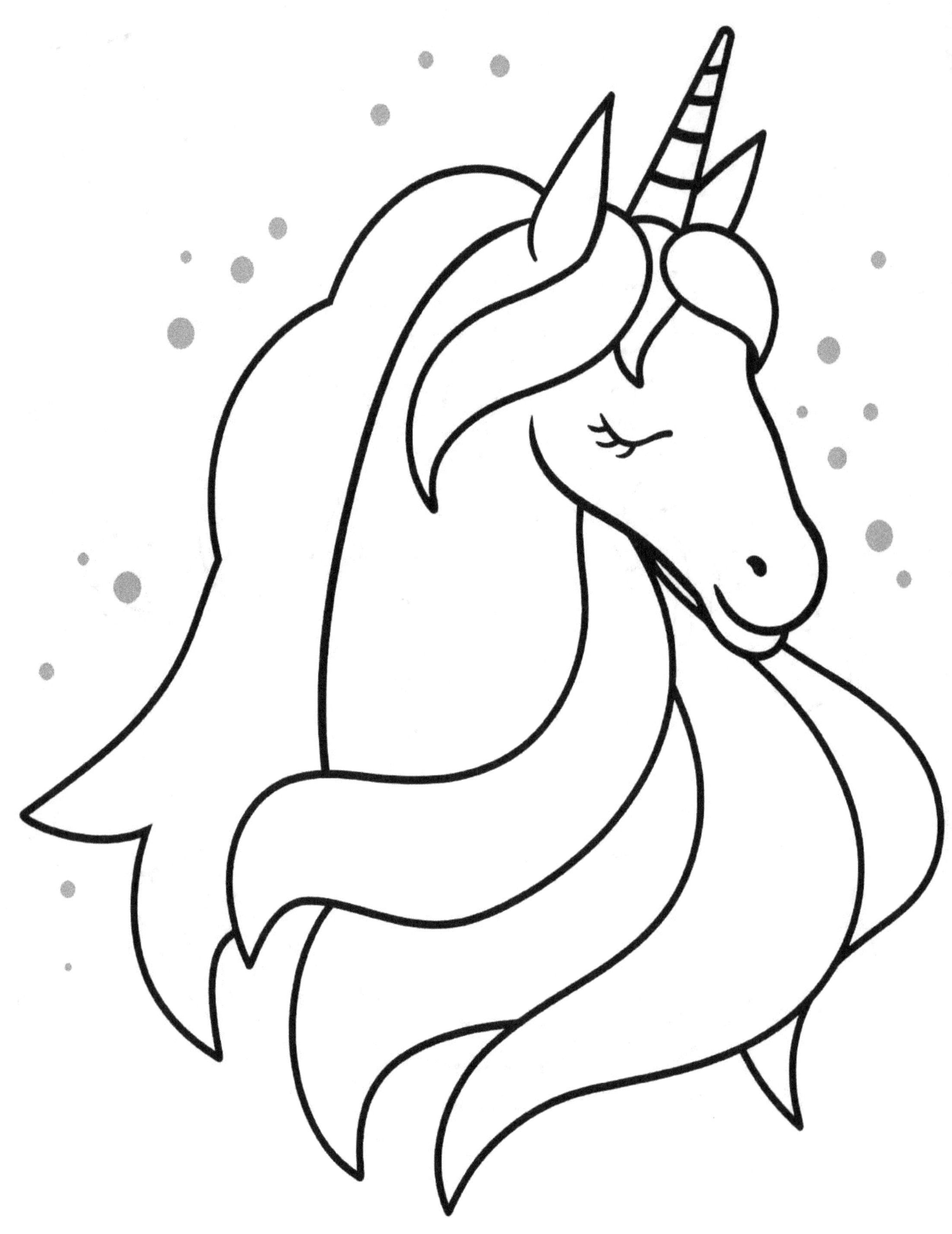

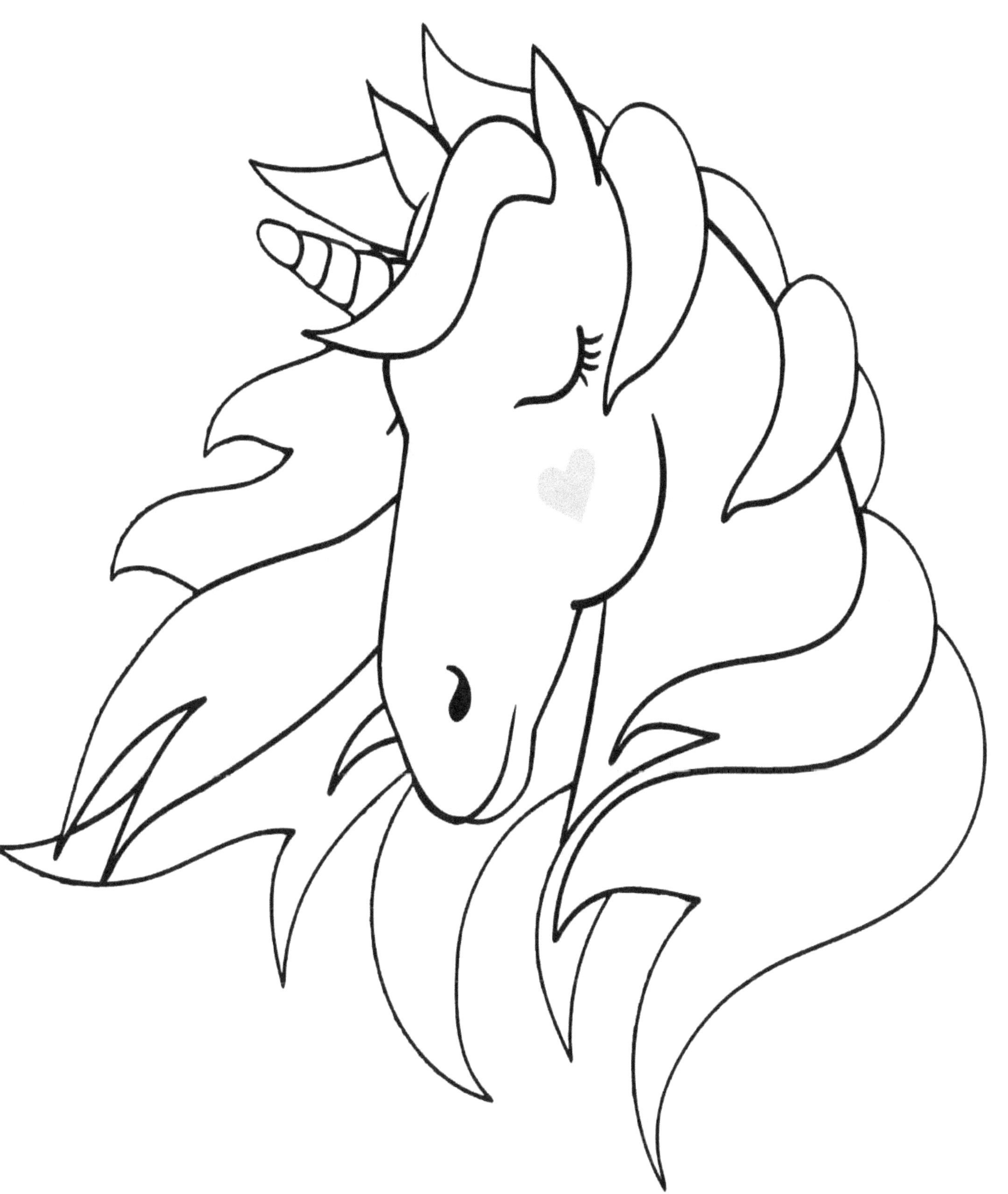

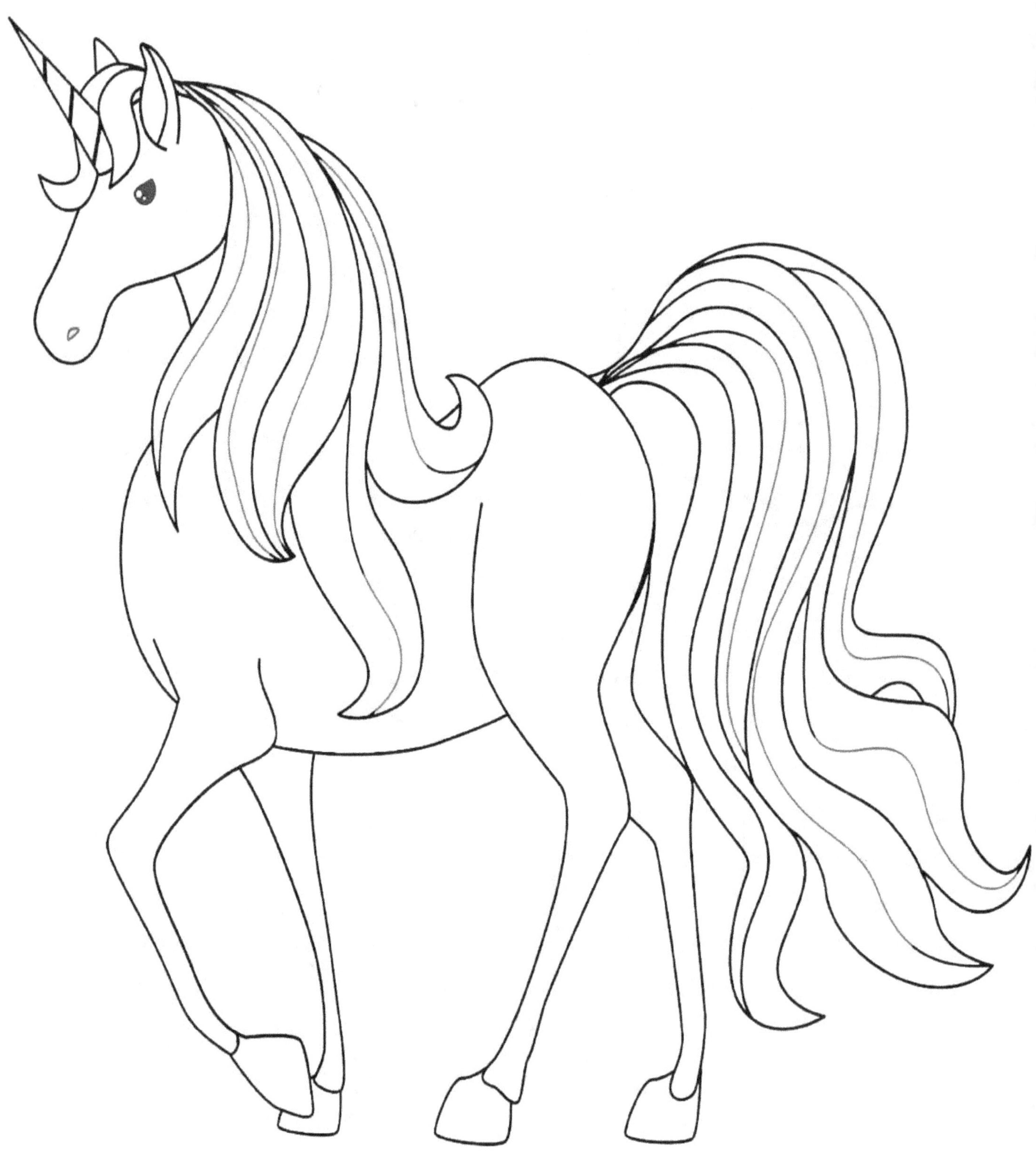

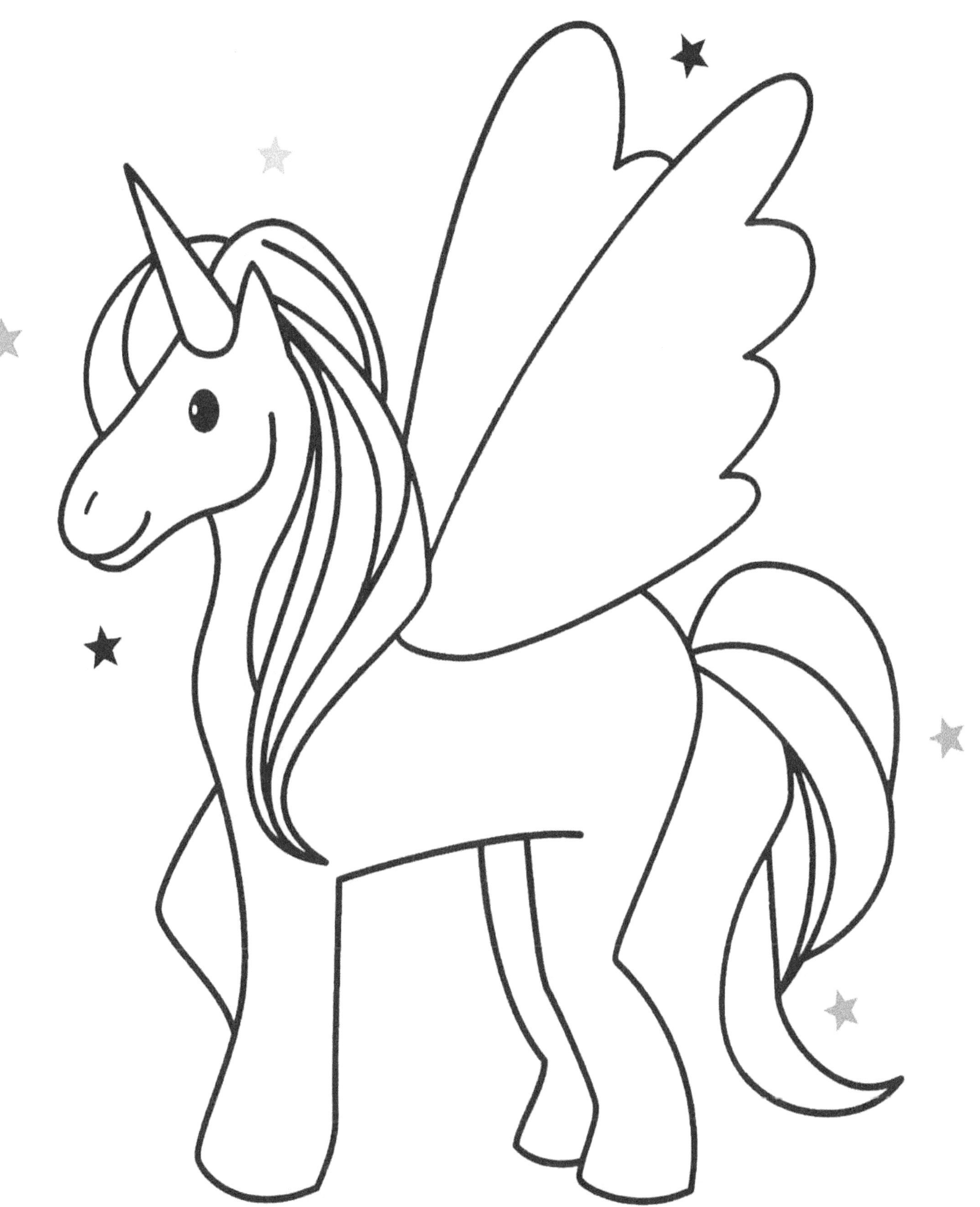

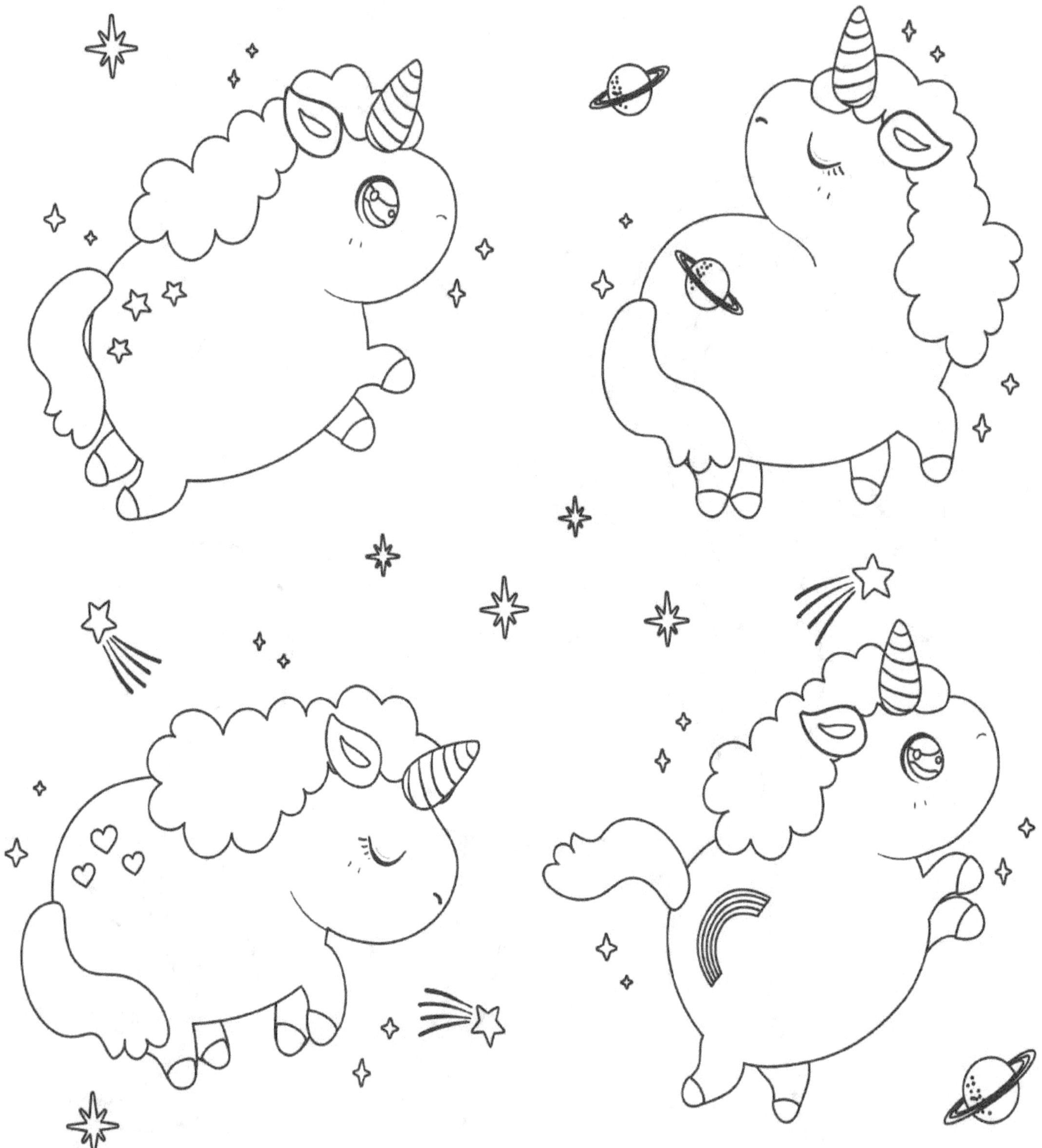

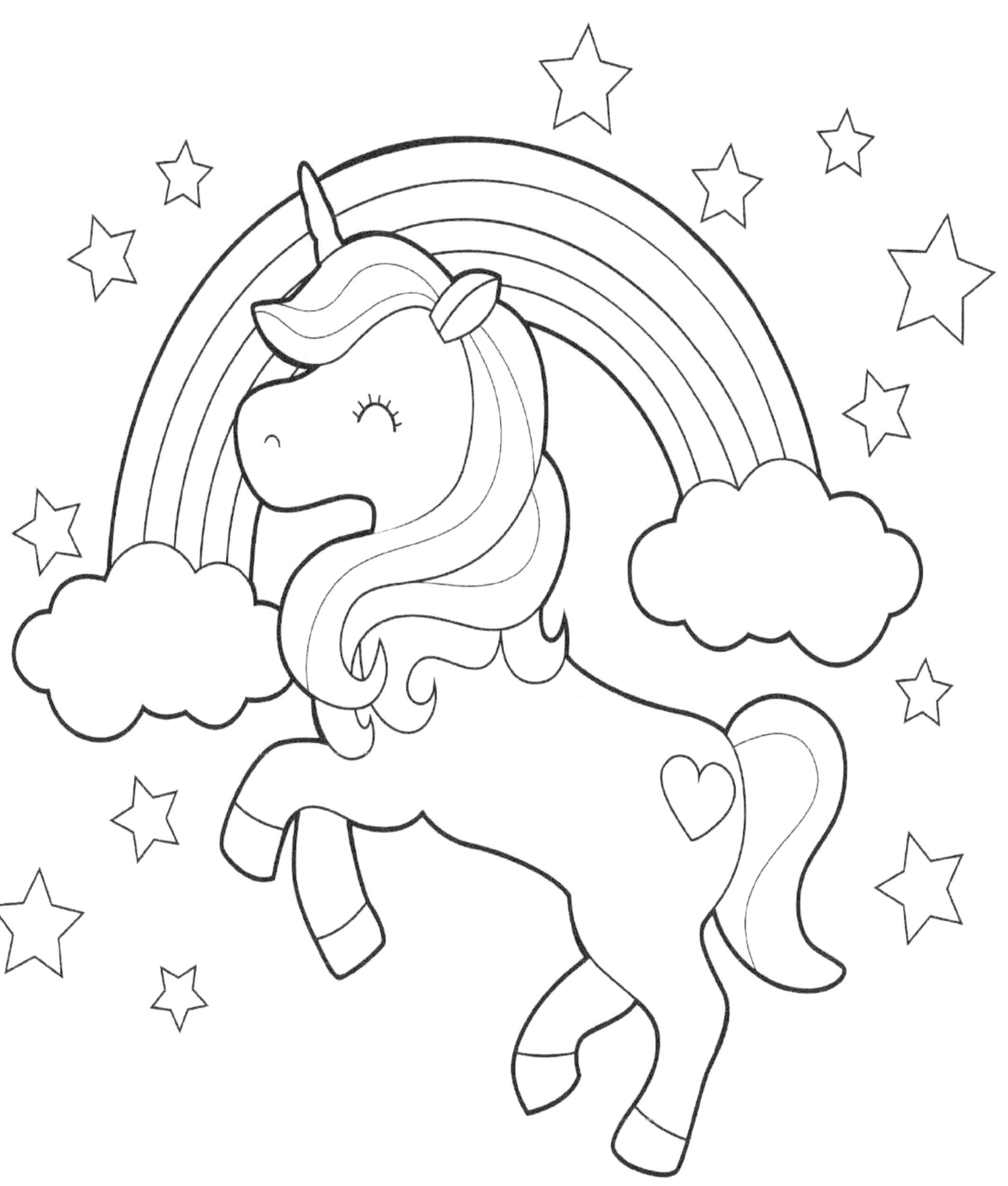

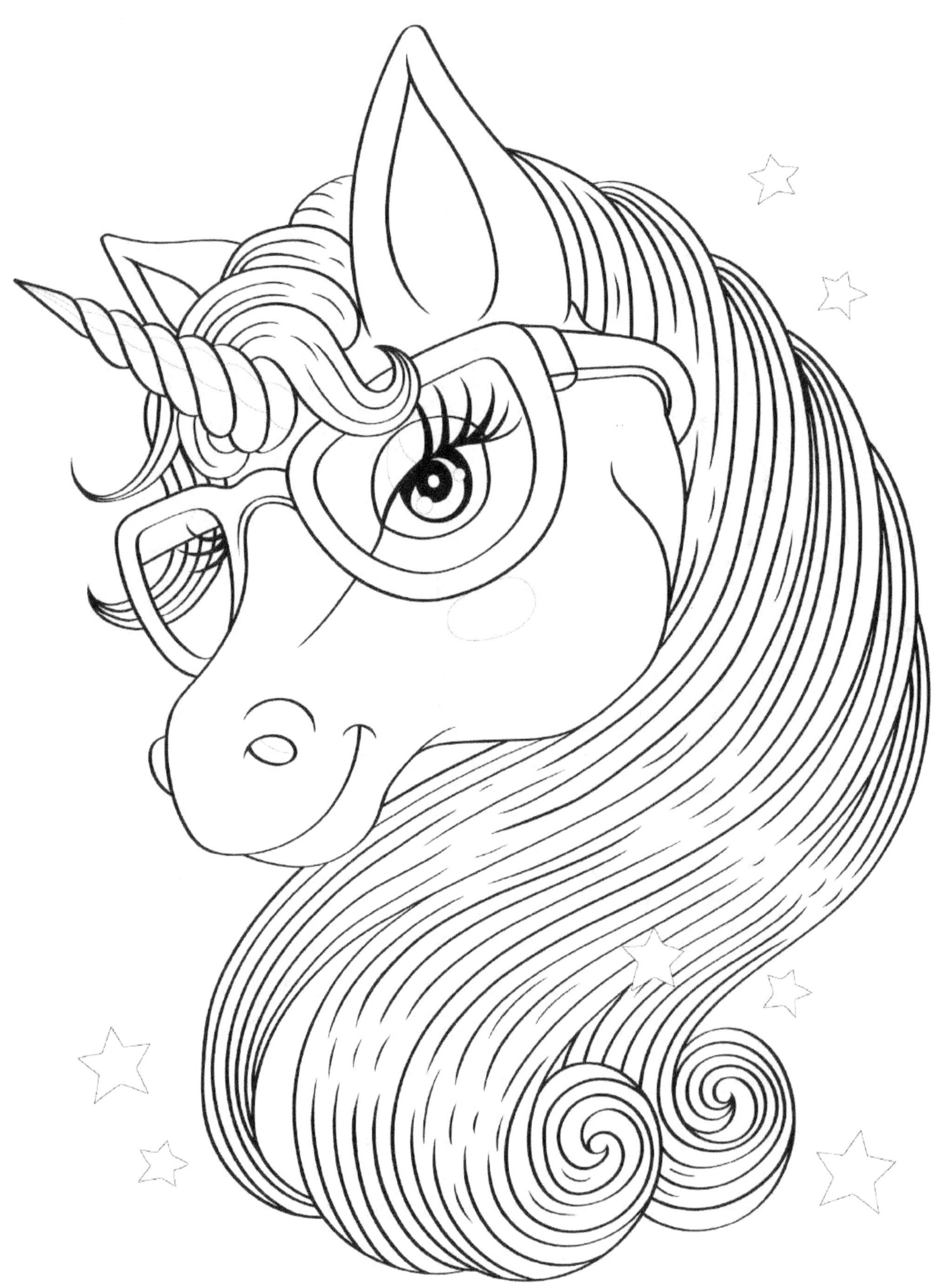

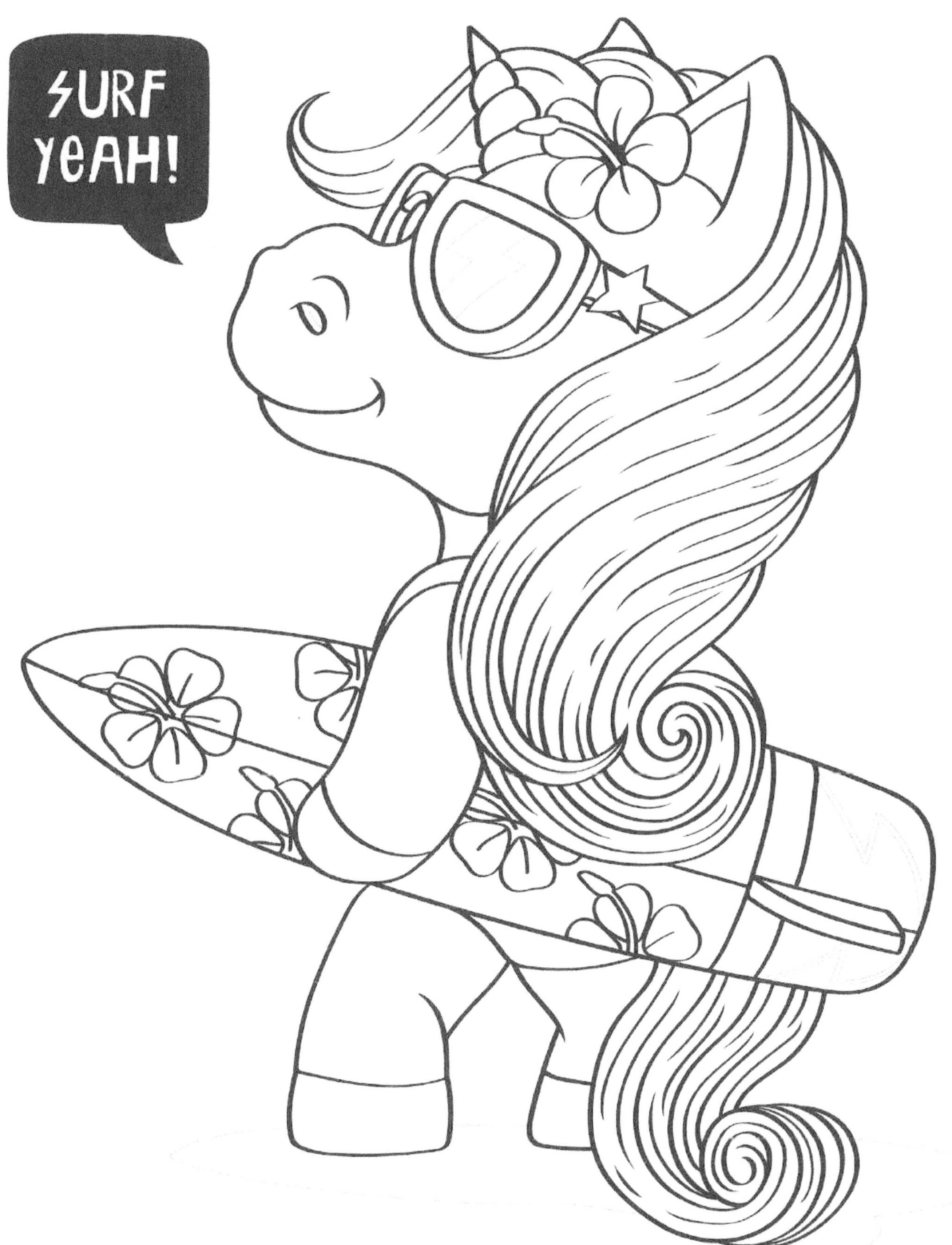
SURF YEAH!